degas to matisse

Impressionist and Modern Masterworks

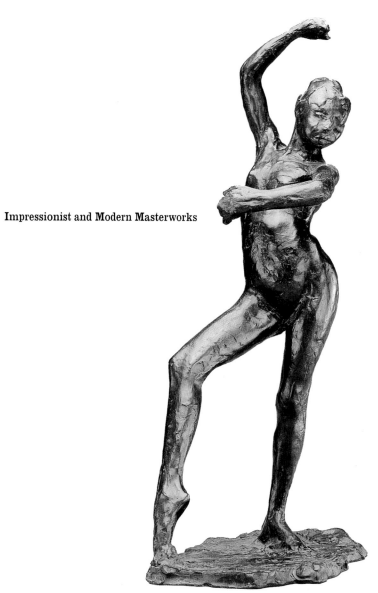

degas to matisse

Impressionist and Modern Masterworks

MERRELL in association with

The Phillips Collection

Ford Motor Company

THE EXHIBITION IS MADE POSSIBLE BY FORD MOTOR COMPANY

Published on the occasion of the exhibition

Degas to Matisse: Impressionist and Modern Masterworks from The Detroit Institute of Arts

at The Phillips Collection, Washington, D.C.
September 23, 2000 –
January 21, 2001

The exhibition is organized by The Phillips Collection

in cooperation with

The Detroit Institute of Arts

First published in 2000 by Merrell Publishers Limited
42 Southwark Street
London SE1 1UN

in association with

The Phillips Collection
1600 Twenty-first Street, N.W.
Washington, D.C. 20009-1090

Produced by
Merrell Publishers Limited
Design and typography in Bayer, Clarendon and Walbaum by
STUDIOGOSSETT
Edited by
Johanna Halford-MacLeod and
Julian Honer
Printed and bound in Italy

Distributed in the USA and Canada by Rizzoli International Publications, Inc. through St Martin's Press, 175 Fifth Avenue, New York, New York 10010

Text copyright © 2000
The Phillips Collection,
Washington, D.C.

"A Taste for Modernism: Robert Hudson Tannahill's Compatriots and Colleagues" copyright © 2000 Karen Wilkin

"Robert Hudson Tannahill and Duncan Phillips: Collectors and Patrons" copyright © 2000 Stephen Bennett Phillips

"Robert Hudson Tannahill: Some Personal Reminiscences" copyright © 2000 Charles H. Sawyer

Illustrations of works of art from The Detroit Institute of Arts, and photographs of Robert Tannahill and his home copyright © The Detroit Institute of Arts

Illustrations of works of art from The Phillips Collection, and photographs of Duncan Phillips and his home copyright © The Phillips Collection, Washington, D.C.

Library of Congress Cataloging-in-Publication Data

Degas to Matisse: Impressionist and Modern Masterworks
p. cm.
Catalog of an exhibition held at the Phillips Collection, Washington, D.C., Sept. 23, 2000 – Jan. 21, 2000
Includes bibliographical references.
ISBN 1-85894-117-2

1. Modernism (Art) – Exhibitions.
2. Art, Modern – 19th century – Exhibitions.
3. Art, Modern – 20th century – Exhibitions.
4. Tannahill, Robert Hudson – Art collections – Exhibitions.
5. Art – private collections – Michigan – Detroit – Exhibitions.
6. Detroit Institute of Arts – Exhibitions.
7. Phillips, Duncan, 1886–1966 – Art collections – Exhibitions.
8. Art – Private collections – Washington (D.C.) – Exhibitions.
9. Phillips Collection – Exhibitions.
10. Art – Collectors and collecting – United States – History – 20th century – Exhibitions.
I. Phillips Collection.
II. Detroit Institute of Arts.
N6494.M64 D44 2000
709'.041'074753 – dc21
00-055046

British Library Cataloguing-in-Publication Data

Phillips, Stephen Bennett, 1962–
Degas to Matisse : Impressionist and Modern Masterworks
1. Phillips, Duncan, 1886–1966 – Art collections
2. Tannahill, Robert – Art collections
3. Phillips Collection
4. Impressionism (Art)
I. Title
II. Sawyer, Charles
III. Wilkin, Karen
708.1'53

FRONT JACKET
Emil Nolde, *Tulips and Bird,*
c. 1920, (DETAIL; SEE PAGE 126)

BACK JACKET: TOP
Hilaire-Germain-Edgar Degas,
Dancers at the Bar, c. 1900,
(DETAIL; SEE PAGE 83)

BACK JACKET: BOTTOM
Henri Matisse, *Poppies, c.* 1919,
(DETAIL; SEE PAGE 131)

HALF TITLE
Hilaire-Germain-Edgar Degas,
Spanish Dancer, 1900, bronze,
43.2 × 17.2 × 21.9 cm
(17 × 6³⁄₄ × 8⁹⁄₁₆ in.)
THE DETROIT INSTITUTE OF ARTS
GIFT OF ROBERT H. TANNAHILL

FRONTISPIECE
Vincent van Gogh, *Bank of the Oise at Auvers,* 1890,
(DETAIL; SEE PAGE 88)

Contents

Sponsor's Statement

All of us who live and work in Detroit know that
The Detroit Institute of Arts (DIA) is one of our city's
jewels. But we may be less familiar with the individuals
who over the years have made the museum what it is
today. Robert Tannahill is one such man; thanks to his
vision and generosity Detroit is home to an internationally renowned collection of Impressionist and
modern paintings. *Degas to Matisse* is the first exhibition
held outside Detroit that focuses on the remarkable
masterpieces collected by Robert H. Tannahill and
donated to the DIA, where they are the object of our
great admiration and affection.

Tannahill's legacy mirrors our own aspirations at
Ford Motor Company. We are committed to being a
leader in our community and in the world. We believe
in the power of art to inspire originality and ingenuity
in all walks of life. We work to enrich the quality of life
in the cities and countries where we do business by
investing in the long-term growth of our cultural and
educational institutions.

On behalf of the 400,000 employees of Ford worldwide,
I would like to thank the trustees and staff of The
Phillips Collection for organizing this magnificent
exhibition. It is a special privilege to be able to share the
artistic treasures of Detroit with residents and visitors in
our nation's capital.

William Clay Ford Jr.
Chairman
Ford Motor Company

Foreword

The United States is home to an esteemed community of art museums. Bequeathed to us in the nineteenth century by Europe, where large-scale collecting has enjoyed a long history, the museum as a repository for works of art and precious objects ultimately found the American climate to be surprisingly sympathetic. By the early years of the twentieth century a growing community of American museums, with the name of the appropriate city chiseled over the door, raised expectations for a nation previously undistinguished for important collecting or even for paying attention to its home-grown artists.

It is now, to a remarkable extent, a feature characteristic of American urban life to enjoy the benefits of public museums known for collections that are wide and deep — collections that have been built over a remarkably short period of time and that have in turn generated audiences that are large and loyal.

At the foundation of this success lies a tradition of inspired personal collecting informed by a sense of public responsibility and generosity. Even the largest and greatest of the art museums in this country would be rendered unrecognizable by the removal of a handful of the names of individuals and families whose vision and generosity have shaped many much-loved public institutions.

The present exhibition focuses on Robert Hudson Tannahill of Detroit. Tannahill is remembered by those who knew him as a serious, somewhat retiring figure, whose collection of nineteenth- and twentieth-century painting, sculpture, and works on paper forms the core of the modern department at The Detroit Institute of Arts. Tannahill collected in many fields — in subjects as remote from each other as French decorative arts and African sculpture — and he benefited the museum in each of these areas. But it is in his commitment to modern art and to finding for it a public forum that he engages us here — particularly in the context of another major collector, Duncan Phillips. Tannahill worked within the context of a large institution, The Detroit Institute of Arts, a superb example of the comprehensive American museum with stellar collections that grew with its community, just as did the major museums in such cities as Philadelphia, Cleveland, or Kansas City. Phillips pursued his own path in Washington before the Mall was lined with major museums. In the process, he created America's first museum of modern art.

Seen in the context of each other's accomplishments, the similarities of their collecting are striking, although the differences are perhaps even more so. But of greatest importance is that, in the case of both these men, the public was to become their beneficiary. Great institutions are indeed created by great citizens. In support of that proposition we offer the following narrative of lives informed by a love of great art, the judgment to discern it, and the generosity to place it in the public trust.

Jay Gates
Director
The Phillips Collection

Graham W.J. Beal
Director
The Detroit Institute of Arts

Acknowledgments

Degas to Matisse: Impressionist and Modern Masterworks from The Detroit Institute of Arts provides the opportunity to compare two great American collectors of modern art: Duncan Phillips and Robert H. Tannahill. The one in Washington, D.C., the other in Detroit, both shared a passion for works of art and for educating the public about modernism. Their desire to understand and communicate the aesthetic awakenings of their time led them to acquire superb works of art that, in turn, vastly enhanced American museum holdings. Many of the works that Duncan Phillips purchased for The Phillips Collection bear a striking resemblance in terms of artist and subject-matter to pieces that Robert H. Tannahill acquired for his collection and eventually gave to The Detroit Institute of Arts. In addition to exploring the similarities as well as the differences in the personal collecting tastes of these two men, this publication sheds light on the rich tapestry of American collectors who acquired European and American modern art in the first half of the twentieth century. In doing so, it increases our understanding of the choices that Duncan Phillips made as he built his "museum of modern art and its sources."

Major financial support was essential to organizing this exhibition. The Phillips Collection is immensely grateful to our sponsor, Ford Motor Company. Ford's strong and early commitment made *Degas to Matisse: Impressionist and Modern Masterworks from The Detroit Institute of Arts* possible.

The Phillips Collection is also tremendously grateful to our colleagues at The Detroit Institute of Arts for their willingness to work with us on this project. In particular, we would like to thank the museum's former Interim Director, Maurice D. Parrish, who was instrumental in the initial planning of the exhibition, and its present Director, Graham W.J. Beal, who has continued to support the project enthusiastically. We owe special thanks to David Penney, Chief Curator, for his manifold assistance, as well as to George S. Keyes, Curator of European Paintings, Ellen Sharp, Curator of Graphic Arts, and MaryAnn Wilkinson, Curator of Twentieth-Century Art, for their thoughtfulness in refining the checklist and their willingness to allow these key works of art from the collection to travel to Washington. Tara Robinson, Curator of Exhibitions, and Pamela Watson, Head Registrar, were invaluable in helping to coordinate the exhibition. In addition, this publication would not be possible without the help of Sylvia Inwood, who provided transparencies and black-and-white photographs of works from the Tannahill collection, and William H. Peck, Senior Curator, who carefully read the essays.

Many individuals have contributed their time and energy to the exhibition catalogue. We are particularly grateful to Karen Wilkin for her overview of several key American collectors in the first half of the twentieth century, which provides a framework for our understanding of the world in which Duncan Phillips and Robert H. Tannahill were collecting. We are delighted that Charles H. Sawyer was able to give us a wonderful personal account of his memories of Tannahill as well as an insightful comparison of these two extraordinary individuals. We are grateful to Susan Wyman and William A. Bostick for their assistance with Charles Sawyer's manuscript, and to Lisa Siegrist and Donald Garfield for the excellent job they did editing the entire volume. We also appreciate the support of Merrell Publishers, especially Hugh Merrell.

The entire staff of The Phillips Collection has contributed to this exhibition and catalogue. Director, Jay Gates, and Senior Curator, Elizabeth Hutton Turner, were involved in the early planning stage of this project. Special thanks are due to Joseph Holbach, Chief Registrar, Linda Clous, Assistant Registrar, and Thora Colot, Director of Marketing and Business Activities. I would especially like to acknowledge Johanna Halford-MacLeod, Programming and Publications Director, for her hard work on this book, and her team of volunteers – Guy Halford-MacLeod, Sandy Schlachtmeyer, and Helen Thomas – who contributed a great deal. Above all, I would like to acknowledge the dedication of Stephen Bennett Phillips, Associate Curator, who has organized the exhibition for The Phillips Collection and worked so hard on its realization.

Eliza E. Rathbone
Chief Curator
The Phillips Collection

Constantin Brancusi

(1876–1957)

Sleeping Child, c. 1906–08

SEE PAGE 70

A Taste for Modernism:

Karen Wilkin

The story of how modernist art came to be accepted in
this country is the story of a few engaged, perhaps
obsessed, forward-looking individuals. Their taste was
often at odds with the accepted norms of their time, but in
the end their passion changed the aesthetic climate of the
U.S. for ever. Part of the credit for introducing Americans
to modernist art must go to the painters and sculptors who
first grasped the implications of European innovations,
and part must go, as well, to a handful of brave dealers
who first showed vanguard art in the U.S. But the
dramatic expansion of American taste that began in the
early part of the twentieth century and whose effects,
for better or worse, are still with us, is also enormously
indebted to the small audience who responded
enthusiastically to what these artists and dealers offered.
An even smaller coterie within this audience is owed
special thanks – the American collectors who felt
compelled to acquire and live with modernist works.

They were a diverse group, linked by their shared open-
mindedness and intelligence, spiced with a certain
amount of willful eccentricity. All of them had sufficient
leisure and means to cultivate their most arcane interests
and the confidence to follow their inclinations. All were
"true collectors," as defined by the art dealer André
Emmerich: people who continue to acquire works of art
after all the walls are filled. What drove them often

Georges Seurat

View of Le Crotoy from

Upstream, 1889

(DETAIL; SEE PAGE 27)

remains mysterious. Only a few kept journals or wrote memoirs describing their pursuit of desired objects. Many were notably reticent, leaving us to speculate about why they embraced – or failed to embrace – particular works by particular artists. Some seem to have acquired what they did solely for their own pleasure; others saw themselves as proselytizers for advanced art. Some seem to have been guided mainly by personal preference; others took advantage of the advice and the exacting eyes of artist friends and fellow aficionados. A small number specialized in a single aspect of modernism, creating significant, focused surveys such as the collections of geometric abstraction and twentieth-century American art at the heart of the present Guggenheim and Whitney museums. Yet collectors who mixed European and American vanguard art (even arbitrarily) may ultimately have had more impact on the evolution of American taste, since these eclectic combinations bridged the perceived gap between Old World and New World culture, opening the way for a notion of parity between them.[1]

Today, many of these American originals – Barnes, Phillips, Whitney, Guggenheim, and Neuberger – are probably better known as the names of important public institutions than as individuals, while some of their colleagues – Dr. Claribel and Miss Etta Cone, for example – are recognized chiefly from exhibition labels and catalogues acknowledging their contributions to museums in the cities where they lived. Still, a handful of American collectors achieved a kind of personal fame. The aura of such pioneers as John Quinn or Gertrude and Leo Stein as legendary supporters of radical art in the early, heroic days of the modernist adventure continues to illuminate the works they once owned. Matisse's *Woman with a Hat* (1905, San Francisco

Museum of Modern Art), the brilliantly colored, audacious portrait so disliked by visitors to the 1905 Salon des Indépendants, has entered the history of art both as an icon of Fauvism and as the first of Matisse's works purchased by the Steins. Similarly, his *Blue Nude: Memory of Biskra* (1907, Baltimore Museum of Art), with its clenched pose and thrusting hip, is famous both as a reinvention of Michelangelo's *Dawn* from the Medici Chapel, Florence, and as a picture whose pedigree can be traced from the artist to Leo Stein to John Quinn to the Cone sisters. The original owners of other important modernist works are often less easily recognized. Yet even though the names of such retiring, but enthusiastic, collectors as Earl Horter and Robert H. Tannahill are familiar mainly to connoisseurs and art historians researching provenances, they, too, were invaluable in helping Americans to take the art of their own time seriously.

Today, it can be difficult to realize how daring these collectors were. Not only are the paintings and sculptures they acquired greatly admired and often extravagantly valued, but their modern counterparts are greatly admired, too. Seen as specially perceptive and in tune with the times, they are courted by dealers and museums, flattered by the art press, and offered entrée into circles regarded as chic and desirable. Today, collecting new, even outrageous, art can burnish an image in the way that collecting the art of the past could a century ago, a remarkable shift when we consider that, for newly rich American industrialists of the Gilded Age, only the acquisition of Old Masters was guaranteed to enhance status; an interest in contemporary art conferred no such benefit, unless it was having one's portrait painted by an accepted master such as John Singer Sargent. Quite the contrary: the patron of unconventional artists of his own day was regarded with suspicion and hostility. Only Impressionism, of all modern painting movements, was welcomed early on in this country, which explains the large number of fine Impressionist works now in U.S. museums.

The collection assembled by the sugar baron H.O. Havemeyer (1847–1907) and his wife Louisine (1855–1929), now divided among the Metropolitan Museum, New York, the National Gallery, Washington, and the Shelburne Museum, Shelburne, VT, is both typical and atypical of what a New York couple of immense means and taste would have acquired between the 1880s and the first part of the twentieth century.[2] Its Italian, Dutch, and Spanish Old Masters and its French nineteenth-century masterpieces, Asian art, and decorative objects seem distinguished mainly by their excellence. But the collection also includes impressive numbers of important works by Cézanne, Degas, Manet, and Monet, acquired, for the most part, during the artists' lifetimes. Louisine Elder Havemeyer was a close friend of Mary Cassatt, who was not only a serious, gifted painter, but also one of Degas's few intimates. On a visit to Paris in 1876, Miss Elder, aged twenty-one, began purchasing contemporary art, acquiring her first Monet, a landscape of 1874, and choosing her first Degas, a pastel of dancers from about 1876, in his studio, introduced and accompanied by Cassatt. Returning to France three years later, Louisine bought a Pissarro and a gouache by Cassatt. Meanwhile, her future husband concentrated on Barbizon School and similar works (later winnowed out of the collection); he also began a lifelong love affair with Japanese ceramics.

After their marriage in 1883, the Havemeyers continued to rely on Cassatt's eye (and, it appears, on Degas's

opinions transmitted by her). Perhaps because Cassatt had educated their taste, throughout the 1890s, the couple remained loyal to the Impressionists, buying Cassatt's and Degas's work out of the studio and purchasing other innovative pictures, including examples of Monet's grainstack and poplar series, soon after they were painted, installing them in their elegant Fifth Avenue house with its Tiffany-designed interiors. But while such choices were certainly progressive – think of the Frick Collection, by contrast – buying Impressionist works, even newly minted ones, in the 1890s was not comparable to the young Louisine's buying a Degas and a Monet two years after the first Impressionist show. Whether because fashionable collectors such as the Havemeyers approved of them or because of their inherent virtues, by the 1890s, Impressionist pictures were so sought after in America that Monet's prestigious Paris dealer, Durand-Ruel, opened a branch in New York.

The Havemeyers continued on occasion to patronize Durand-Ruel, both locally and in France, but after about 1888, for the rest of their life together, they devoted increasing amounts of time and resources to Old Master and earlier nineteenth-century art. They relied less on expert advice than on their own opinions, as though confident that their connoisseurship and aesthetic acuity had been honed by their experience of more recent art, an assumption justified by their acquisition of superb portraits by Rembrandt, Bronzino, and Hugo van der Goes,[3] and important canvases by Corot and Courbet. A trip to Italy and Spain in 1900, seeking treasures from obscure private collections, apparently as much in the hope of bargains as of discoveries, eventually yielded works by Veronese, El Greco, and Goya. (Modern scholarship has downgraded some of these blue-chip attributions, but this applies both to works chosen independently and with advice.) Yet the couple never entirely stopped acquiring Impressionist works, buying an iconic Monet Japanese bridge in 1900, the same year that they trekked through rural Italy in quest of Renaissance portraits. In 1921, about fifteen years after her husband's death, Louisine purchased one of the first sets of posthumous casts of Degas's sculptures, works virtually unknown to anyone outside the intensely private artist's immediate circle, and in 1922, a cast of his *Little Dancer, Fourteen Years Old* (1878–81), which she had longed to own since 1903, when she first saw the deteriorating wax original, "in pieces, in a little vitrine"[4] in his studio.

Nonetheless, while Degas's sculpture appears innovative and provocative, even today, it hardly qualified as radical work in 1921. While the Havemeyers had been buying Impressionist and Old Master paintings, visionary European artists had transformed time-honored conceptions of what a work of art could be, through the free-wheeling explorations now labeled Post-Impressionism, Fauvism, Cubism, and Expressionism. In the years before the First World War, while Louisine Havemeyer was hoping to buy Degas's *Little Dancer*, American artists such as John Marin, Alfred Maurer, Marsden Hartley, Max Weber, and Arthur B. Carles were spending extended periods in Europe, in order to participate first hand in these experiments, as were a few intrepid art lovers.

The best-known collectors from this generation are probably a quartet of cultured, expatriate Americans: Leo and Gertrude Stein (1872–1947 and 1874–1946), their brother Michael (1865–1938), and his wife, Sarah (1870–1953).[5] Their support was invaluable to the young unknowns whose art attracted them, but the Steins were more than patrons; they were insiders who became friends of the artists whose work they bought. Gertrude and Picasso were famously close, while Matisse found the Michael Steins – especially Sarah – particularly sympathetic. Gertrude and Leo's apartment on the rue de Fleurus, (later the home of Gertrude and Alice B. Toklas), with its walls lined with a steadily growing collection of Cézannes, Matisses, Picassos, and Braques, and its tables crowded with sculptures by Matisse, Jacques Lipchitz, and their colleagues, became a salon for the European and expatriate avant garde of Paris, and a place of pilgrimage for visiting Americans. Especially during the heady, early years of Fauvism and Cubism, between about 1905 and the outbreak of the First World War, when Matisse, Picasso, and *la bande à* Picasso were frequent visitors, along with just about every other progressive artist, writer, musician, or aesthete in Paris, Saturday evenings at the rue de Fleurus were essential to the education of anyone interested in new art of any kind – part of their initiation into the mysteries of modernism.[6]

The Steins' influence spread. Introducing their friends from Baltimore, the physician Dr. Claribel Cone

John Marin
(1870–1953)
New Mexican Landscape,
near Taos, 1930
watercolor on paper
35.2 × 47.6 cm
(13⅞ × 18¾ in.)
THE DETROIT INSTITUTE OF ARTS
BEQUEST OF ROBERT H. TANNAHILL

John Marin
(1870–1953)
Mt. Chocorua –
White Mountains, 1926
watercolor and graphite
on paper
42.5 × 54.6 cm
(16¾ × 21½ in.)
Washington, D.C.
The Phillips Collection

(1864–1929) and her musician sister, Etta (1870–1949), to the world of Picasso and Matisse, about 1905, had particularly lasting repercussions.˙ The sisters developed a healthy appetite for modernist art, returning regularly to Paris to make purchases. They became lifelong friends and patrons of Matisse, a relationship that visibly influenced the group of works they gradually put together. The Cone collection became a Matisse retrospective in miniature: more than forty paintings spanning most of his career, from 1895 to 1947, including the celebrated reclining figure *Pink Nude* (1935), with its arabesque contours and geometric

background of blue and white tiles, and more than a dozen sculptures and numerous drawings. Context was provided by works by Matisse's contemporaries – Picasso (represented in some depth), Braque, Derain, Vlaminck, and Bonnard, among others – and by a selection of works by his predecessors, from Delacroix, Courbet, and Corot to Degas, Cézanne, Gauguin, and Van Gogh.

The Steins' role in introducing the Cones to the work of their artist friends was pivotal, but the sisters' rapid, whole-hearted response speaks for their own daring and determination, attributes that colored both of their lives.

John Marin

(1870–1953)

Near Great Barrington, 1925

watercolor and graphite on

paper

38.4 × 47.9 cm

(15⅛ × 18⅞ in.)

Washington, D.C.

The Phillips Collection

Neither fulfilled the standard expectations of the period for women of their affluent, eminently respectable background – apart from serving on the boards of various important institutions, later in life. Neither married. Perhaps most remarkable, Claribel, who studied medicine and pathology at Johns Hopkins and in Germany, held a professorship at the Woman's Medical College in Baltimore as early as the 1890s – unlike her friend Gertrude, who enrolled at Johns Hopkins Medical School, but never finished the course – an indication of courage and perseverance that has been seen as prefiguring the courage that it took for two young women, traveling in Europe in 1905, to spend their allowances on a bizarre, disturbing painting from Matisse's studio. That these independent-minded women were never comfortable with work that verged on abstraction takes nothing away from the fundamentally adventurous nature of the works they chose.

It is impossible to determine the effect of this splendid collection on the Cones' fellow citizens. The sisters lived quietly with their paintings, drawings, and sculptures in the apartment they shared with their brother, shunning publicity but hospitable to interested visitors. A former professor of philosophy at Johns Hopkins, who became the sisters' admiring friend, recalled inquiring about the collection when he first came to Baltimore, in 1921, and being warned that its owners were "beyond doubt mental cases."[8] In spite – or because – of this perception, the Cones decided that their paintings and sculptures should reach a wider audience. When Claribel died in 1929, she left her pictures to Etta with the suggestion that after *her* death, the collection go to the Baltimore Museum. Two decades later, in 1949, when these lovingly assembled works entered the museum, they were eagerly received. During the intervening years, the artists whom the "mental cases" once supported in defiance of general approval had become universally acclaimed. How this came about can never be explained fully, but it must have something to do with the fact that enthusiasts like the Cone sisters helped to accustom American eyes to innovative European art simply by assuring its presence in this country.

The effects of another memorable collector's efforts on the relationship of Americans and modernist art are more easily charted. During the decade and a half between about 1910 and his death, the lawyer-collector-patron John Quinn (1870–1924) was arguably the single essential figure in the nascent American vanguard.[9] Quinn began collecting modernist art when he was approaching forty, after an intense involvement with Irish art and literature; he not only bought the work of Augustus and Gwen John, but also counted them as friends, along with the Yeats family, J.M. Synge, the critic George Russell, and Lady Gregory, whose Abbey Players Quinn sponsored when they toured the U.S. and defended in court when Synge's *Playboy of the Western World* provoked objections. Quinn remained a supporter of new literature, funding Jane Heap and Margaret

Anderson's *Little Review*, which published Stein and James Joyce in America, and providing legal defense (unfortunately without success) when the two women were tried for obscenity, in 1920, for publishing *Ulysses*, in serial form.

Quinn discovered French vanguard art in Paris in 1911 and 1912, possibly steered toward it by his friends, the progressive painters Walter Pach, Walt Kuhn, and Arthur B. Davies, and the critic James Gibbons Huneker, an avid supporter of the controversial American painters who exhibited together as The Eight. Quinn began acquiring works with such enthusiasm that by 1913, when his artist friends helped to organize the vast, controversial International Exhibition of Modern Art, known as the Armory Show, in New York, he was its principal single lender, supplying seventy-nine works by Puvis de Chavannes, Cézanne, Gauguin, Van Gogh, and Augustus and Gwen John. Quinn was also the largest single purchaser from the Armory Show, as well as the exhibition's lawyer.

Quinn seems to have welcomed advice from his American artist and critic friends, and employed, too, the writer Henri Pierre Roché, who was part of the Stein circle, to help locate works for purchase in Paris. Quinn's growing acquaintance with the European artists he most admired may also have influenced his choices, but finally, all decisions about what he acquired or rejected were his alone. His collection reflected both his individual preferences and his increasingly demanding standards. Especially after he was treated for cancer in 1918, Quinn consciously sharpened his focus. "I desire to add only works of first rate importance," he wrote to Marcel Duchamp in 1920.[10] To a remarkable extent, he succeeded, apart from an inexplicable enthusiasm for the sculpture of Raymond Duchamp-Villon. Quinn eventually owned an astonishing number of major works by Brancusi, whom he revered, a group of stellar Matisses – among other outstanding works, the celebrated *Blue Nude* (1907) now in Baltimore, and the enigmatic *Italian Woman* (1915, Solomon R. Guggenheim Museum) – as well as key canvases by Braque, Cézanne, and Gauguin, and more. Quinn's Picassos were equally important, several of them exemplifying the pivotal moment when the fragile Rose Period nudes began to harden into massive precursors of *Les Demoiselles d'Avignon.*

When the Metropolitan Museum organized its first exhibition of modern art, in 1921, it relied heavily on loans from Quinn, but generally he was an intensely private man who collected mainly for his own pleasure and allowed only close friends to view the works in his Central Park West apartment. Yet he left an indelible mark on the American audience for modernist art. Since he saw himself as custodian, rather than owner, of the works he lived with, he left instructions for everything to be sold after his death. The most ambitious collectors of the day – including the Cones, Earl Horter, and Quinn's arch-rival, Barnes – took full advantage of the opportunity, beginning the process of disseminating Quinn's rigorously chosen works to a wider public. Today they figure prominently in public institutions throughout the U.S.

The second part of Quinn's legacy was a legal coup with profound ramifications. In 1913, after the Armory Show, he succeeded in having the U.S. government revoke a punitive import duty imposed since 1909 on recent art. (The tax was justified as "protection" for living American artists; older art came in duty free, which Quinn maintained benefited only those rich enough

to buy Old Masters.) Abolishing the duty paved the way for a host of new galleries dedicated to European and American moderns to open in the wake of the Armory Show, including, among others, Stieglitz's 291, the Daniel Gallery, Stephan Bourgeois, and de Zayas's Modern Gallery (even the staid, established Montross and Knoedler galleries began to show modern art after about 1913), vastly enlarging the possibilities for understanding and assimilating the modernist experiment for American artist and spectators alike.

Advanced art was still ignored by American museums and regarded with skepticism, if at all, by most people, but a gradual erosion of such prejudices was begun by this burst of activity. Many current institutions were born in these formative years. In 1914, Gertrude Vanderbilt Whitney created the Whitney Studio Club for young, progressive artists; membership requirements of five dollars annually and talent provided access to galleries, studios, a library, and a meeting room near her 8th Street sculpture studio. The works Mrs. Whitney purchased from exhibitions held at the Club formed the nucleus of the future Whitney Museum of American Art. In 1920, two years before Louisine Havemeyer acquired her much-desired Degas sculpture of the little dancer, the Société Anonyme, the direct ancestor of the Museum of Modern Art, was founded by Katherine Dreier, Marcel Duchamp, and Man Ray. In 1927, the Gallatin collection of modern art went on view at New York University. Two years later, in 1929, the Museum of Modern Art opened in a townhouse on 53rd Street – all essential steps in educating American audiences about what to look for (and not look for) in modernist art.

The process was accelerated by the efforts of collectors who saw themselves as missionaries for the avant garde.

The most serious of these was unquestionably Albert Barnes (1872–1951), who regarded his collection as material for an ambitious experiment in education.[11] Barnes's story is well known: an eccentric, cantankerous chemist, who rose from poverty to great wealth, he assembled one of this country's great collections of modernist paintings, and in 1925 opened a museum notorious for being difficult to get into and idiosyncratically organized. The cranky rules that forbade the loan of works to exhibitions or (until recently) their reproduction in color are also familiar. What is less known is that the Barnes Foundation's famously peculiar galleries, with their pictures arranged according to formal and aesthetic relationships, rather than chronological or historical ones, were (and still are) used as a laboratory for very specialized courses of study.

Barnes began collecting in the early 1900s, as soon as he became successful, and just as soon began using pictures as educational tools. Inspired by such theorists as William James, Bertrand Russell, John Dewey, and George Santayana on intelligence, thinking, and the perception of beauty, Barnes hung paintings by American moderns, including Glackens, Prendergast, and Maurer, in his factory, making them the center of discussion groups with his workers. By the early 1910s, Barnes had both expanded his experiments with education and social action, and begun to collect French modernist painting with single-minded intensity. At first, like Quinn, he valued – but by no means followed –

the recommendations of such artists as Glackens, a friend from his impoverished Philadelphia childhood, and Maurer, a member of the Steins' circle in Paris, but he ultimately dispensed entirely with advisers. Although he remained close to Glackens, Barnes preferred to travel regularly to Paris and rely entirely on his own aesthetic judgment, although he certainly must have benefited from his growing friendship with the astute Leo Stein.

By 1914, Barnes owned, by his count, twenty-five Renoirs, twelve Cézannes, and twelve Picassos,[12] the core of the fascinating, quirky collection that today is still on view in the elegant Paul Cret building Barnes commissioned for it in 1922. Through discerning (and sometimes purely willful) purchases and trades, the collection expanded to include exemplary works by Seurat, Gauguin, Van Gogh, Modigliani, Toulouse-Lautrec, and Braque, as well as more Picassos, but its greatest strength remains its extraordinary pieces by Cézanne and Matisse. The Cézannes range from intimate, vigorous groups of bathers to one of the most ambitious and austere of the card players, while the Matisses include such legendary works as the seminal, problematic *Le Bonheur de vivre* (1905–06), which announces the painter's concerns for virtually the rest of his career, and the glorious mural of heroic, sinuous nudes, *The Dance (Merion Dance Mural)* (1931–32), specially commissioned for the space. All of this was installed among specimens of medieval wrought iron, the forms of which, Barnes believed, had affinities with

Pierre-Auguste Renoir

(1841–1919)

The Luncheon of the Boating Party, 1880–81

oil on canvas

130 × 201 cm

(51¼ × 69⅛ in.)

WASHINGTON, D.C.

THE PHILLIPS COLLECTION

his modernist pictures, along with African sculpture, the occasional Native American artifact, and a staggering number of Renoirs of distinctly uneven quality.

Around 1915, Barnes began to write about art, the start of a series of essays that became fundamental texts for the notably hermetic courses taught at the Foundation, which were designed to encourage wider understanding of formal and aesthetic principles of art (as conceived by Barnes) through the study of the works in the collection. In one of his early essays, "How to Judge a Painting," published in *Arts and Decoration*, Barnes praised the Havemeyer collection as "the best and wisest" in America because of its strong concentration of works by "the Frenchmen of about 1860 and later, whose work is so richly expressive of life that means most to the normal man alive today."[13] Barnes's desire to make his treasures intelligible to "the normal man alive today" produced a strangely exclusive institution that added mystery and desirability to the works of art it contained, which may, paradoxically, have accelerated their acceptance and appreciation.

By contrast, The Phillips Collection,[14] which opened in 1921, a year before the Barnes Foundation was created, was conceived from the start as a public institution – the first museum of modern art in America – a monument to Duncan Phillips's art-loving father and older brother, who died within thirteen months of each other. Excellence was the main criterion, with key artists collected in groups to show their evolution, and others included to demonstrate relationships and influences, or alternative directions. A sense of the whole and of mission seems always to have influenced choices.

The museum's sole Renoir, the enchanting *Luncheon of the Boating Party* (1880–81; see illus., p. 21), with its youthful holiday-makers at a riverside restaurant, was purchased in 1923 for its beauty, size, and importance within the painter's œuvre, specifically to draw attention to the fledgling collection.

Duncan Phillips (1886–1966), the heir to a steel, banking, and glass fortune, majored in English at Yale and published his first book, *The Enchantment of Art*, in 1914. Two years later, he and his brother persuaded their father to provide them with an art purchasing fund. When Phillips began buying for his museum, he was audacious from the start, demonstrating a breadth of taste almost unparalleled among American collectors, perhaps because of his avowed public aim. In the 1920s, his acquisitions included works by Chardin, Manet, Monet, and Courbet, along with important American Impressionist and Ashcan School pictures. Over the succeeding decades, Phillips became steadily bolder, focusing on work of his own time, acquiring superlative canvases by Braque and such forward-looking Americans as Demuth, Dove, Marin, Maurer, and Prendergast. The Doves were the first to be purchased by an American museum director, a record maintained with Bonnard, de Staël, and Avery. The Bonnards, which are among the collection's jewels, form an unforgettable group, unique in this country, that reveals how radiant, inventive, and consistent this painter can be; the Braques are similarly choice. Perceptive as his acquisitions of European modernist works were – outstanding canvases by Cézanne, Mondrian, and Matisse, among others – Phillips's most prescient choices may have been in American art, as, for example, when he divided Jacob

Pierre-Auguste Renoir

(1841–1919)

The Palm Tree, 1902

oil on canvas

46.4 × 55.6 cm

(18¼ × 21⅞ in.)

THE DETROIT INSTITUTE OF ARTS

BEQUEST OF ROBERT H. TANNAHILL

Lawrence's wrenching, sixty-panel *The Migration of the American Negro* (1940–41) with the Museum of Modern Art. That Phillips's wife, Marjorie Acker, an equal partner in the formation of the collection, was a serious painter and the niece of the artist Gifford Beal, also influenced the direction and quality of the museum's acquisitions.

Phillips's early perspicacity is noteworthy, but even more impressive is the way the collection developed. Paintings were deaccessioned, given to institutions, or traded to fill holes in the collection, expand its scope, or refine existing selections. Most crucial was the way Phillips's eye evolved to keep pace with the artists to whom he was committed, as their work changed, and with new developments. Most collectors of contemporary art tend to be most comfortable with the work of a particular generation, usually their own. Phillips's taste expanded to include artists young enough to be his children. He acquired significant pictures by Pollock, Motherwell, Gottlieb, Rothko, Noland, and Louis, and a de Kooning, *Asheville* (1949), that remains a touchstone of his work.

If Phillips occupies a special place among the public-spirited collectors of his generation, his opposite number might be Philadelphia's Earl Horter (1880–1940),[15] who feverishly pursued audacious European and American modernist art solely for his own delight. Unlike the affluent, patrician Phillips, Horter was a commercial artist, albeit a highly successful one, who also painted seriously. The contrast between Horter's tame, perceptually based commercial work and his other efforts, which rehearse the innovations of the artists he admired and collected, is striking; as an illustrator, he was accomplished and conventional, but in his paintings,

he was capable of treating the tower of Philadelphia's City Hall the way Delaunay treated the Eiffel Tower.

Like Quinn and Barnes, Horter was close to a group of enlightened artists, who included Sheeler, Franklin Watkins, and especially the sophisticated Arthur B. Carles, when they all lived and worked in Philadelphia. While his friendship and lively discussions with these colleagues must have influenced his aesthetic, Horter's first venture into collecting modernist art dates from the period when he was a novice illustrator-etcher working in New York; he purchased a suite of Vuillard's lithographs from the Armory Show. By the early 1920s, Horter had acquired the first of what would be many splendid Cubist works by Picasso and Braque, and he had discovered Brancusi, perhaps guided by Carles, who was close to the sculptor. These acquisitions seem to have determined the direction of the collection. Over the next decade or so, with enthusiasm verging on obsession, Horter concentrated on the work of these artists, as well as a select group of their colleagues, including Matisse, Gris, and de Chirico, and some vanguard Americans, including his friends Sheeler, Watkins, and Carles, most of them linked by their exploration of Fauvist and Cubist notions of color and form. The resulting collection was at once uncompromising and engagingly personal. Among the most spectacular additions were six works purchased at the 1927 sale of Quinn's art: two Brancusi sculptures, a Braque, a Sheeler, the first version of Duchamp's notorious *Nude Descending a Staircase* (1911, Philadelphia Museum of Art), and Matisse's mysterious *Italian Woman* of 1915, now in the Guggenheim. African and Native American art provided a counterpoint to the modernist gems in Horter's modest apartment, as they did at the Barnes Foundation – where Horter and some of his artist friends, improbably enough, enrolled in one of the classes taught by Barnes. But where Barnes was conspicuously unengaged by the spatial complexities of Analytic Cubism, Horter was both fascinated by its implications and able to single out superlative examples of the idiom.

Like Quinn, Horter appears to have derived enormous pleasure from living with his collection, but he was generous about loans and about having his artist friends profit from first-hand encounters with the art he loved. Sadly, in his last five years, financial difficulties and failing health forced him to sell most of the works he had so passionately assembled. Just as Horter made important purchases from the sale of Quinn's collection, such connoisseurs as the critic Douglas Cooper and the dealer Pierre Matisse made discerning selections from Horter's holdings. Many of his collection's choicest works, such as Picasso's *Portrait of Daniel-Henry Kahnweiler* (1910, Art Institute of Chicago), are now dispersed internationally in museums and private collections, celebrated as emblems of the Cubist enterprise.

The history of Robert H. Tannahill's life (1893–1969) as a collector synthesizes many aspects of his colleagues' stories.[16] Although he was reported to have selected works entirely on his own, he seems to have profited, at least initially, from the advice of informed eyes. There is evidence that Tannahill's aesthetic education owed a good deal to the presence of the German-born art historian William R. Valentiner in Detroit, after about 1921. Both Valentiner's wide-ranging expertise and his intimate knowledge of German Expressionist art have echoes in his young American friend's collection. Later, Tannahill got to know the energetic New York dealer Edith Halpert, when her artist husband began teaching

in Detroit. Halpert was a tireless champion of avant-garde American art whose stable included, after the mid-1920s, such rising American stars as Stuart Davis and William Zorach, and later, Jacob Lawrence. Halpert also inherited the Stieglitz inner circle – Demuth, Dove, Hartley, Marin, and O'Keeffe – after the 291 gallery closed, yet it is worth noting that, despite his long friendship with Halpert, Tannahill bought works by few of the Downtown Gallery's[17] artists for himself. Instead, he gave most of his attention to European moderns, especially the French and Germans, from the early years of the twentieth century, contextualizing them, like the Cones and Phillips, with examples of their predecessors' work and, like Barnes, with African art. Since Tannahill acquired most of his European modernist works in the 1930s, it is difficult to classify him as a pioneering collector, no matter how independently he arrived at his acquisitions, but his impact on his community and the personal character of the works he chose to live with are singular indeed. Perhaps the most individual aspects of Tannahill's collection are its emphasis on German Expressionism and its concentration on works on paper and sculpture.

If Tannahill, in his private mode, pleased only himself, he acted simultaneously as a responsive public benefactor who was both patron and missionary. In his public role, he bought works for The Detroit Institute of Arts and organized exhibitions that not only brought important European and American modern and contemporary art to his native city, but also fostered local talent.[18] In the late 1940s, Tannahill installed his personal collection in a specially designed house, decorated around his works of art. He apparently never added another piece to this meticulously contrived environment, yet he continued to act as a "true collector" – and sometimes an adventurous one – in his public persona, leaving a double legacy with enormous effect on the cultural life of Detroit.

The histories of early collectors of modernist art raise provocative questions. Were they consistently more prescient than their contemporaries or was there a parallel evolution in their own taste in the course of their activity as collectors? Were these advocates and patrons of modernism educated by living with challenging, unconventional work? The evolution of at least one extraordinary European collection, assembled by a French contemporary of the Havemeyers, suggests that the answer to all these questions is an unequivocal "yes." Auguste Pellerin (1852–1929),[19] the elegant, bearded margarine manufacturer whose portrait Matisse painted in 1917, assembled not one but a series of important collections, each more audacious than the preceding one. He began, like any rich industrialist of the late nineteenth century, by purchasing decorative objects and paintings by fashionable, unexceptionable painters such as Jean-Jacques Henner. When Pellerin discovered Corot, he disposed of his Henners. Corot was, in turn, supplanted by the Impressionists, whose work Pellerin selected perceptively, until he began to concentrate on Manet, acquiring a large number of his finest paintings and drawings, including *The Bar at the Folies-Bergère* (1881–82, London, Courtauld Institute). But even Manet was displaced after Pellerin discovered Cézanne at Vollard's gallery around 1895. The difficult, uningratiating painter was the great passion of the industrialist-collector's life. The Manets were sold. Pellerin gradually acquired more than 150 of Cézanne's most powerful oils, from abrasive, expressionist allegories and portraits from his early years to mature masterpieces

such as the *Large Bathers* (1906) now in the Philadelphia Museum of Art. According to Vollard, Pellerin was the first person to buy one of Cézanne's nudes, which frightened everyone else. He eventually owned so many superb examples of the artist's work that he was the principal lender to the influential Cézanne memorial exhibition of 1907, while his collection was the main source of illustrations for Roger Fry's pioneering monograph. It is a compelling story with few clues but the works themselves, testimony to steadily growing powers of discernment and increasing appetite for the unconventional, the emotionally complex, and the rigorous. Clearly, Pellerin learned from the works he lived with.

Of course, the most fascinating thing about any private collection is its individuality, the evidence of decisions that reveal a personality. The Barnes Foundation, for example, offers an informative mix of brilliant choices and dubious ones. Barnes never wavered from the highest standards of intensity in the many Cézannes he acquired, and he was almost as exacting in his choice of Matisses. But Barnes's Renoirs suggest that quantity, not excellence, was the paramount issue in their selection. Barnes seems to have been timid about Cubism, daring in his understanding of Gauguin and Seurat, and delightfully idiosyncratic in his liking for the work of an obscure but charming Ukrainian Cubist named Gritchenko.

Somehow, the often wholly private efforts of these forward-looking individuals helped to transform works initially perceived as radical and difficult into objects of admiration and pride. Many of the paintings and

Georges Seurat

(1859–1891)

View of Le Crotoy from Upstream, 1889

oil on canvas

70.5 × 86.7 cm

(27¾ × 34⅛ in.)

THE DETROIT INSTITUTE OF ARTS

BEQUEST OF ROBERT H. TANNAHILL

sculptures chosen by these indefatigable lovers of modernism, far from seeming radical or difficult today, are ranked among the treasures of our museums and galleries, forming the basis (or even the entirety) of collections that not only are studied by scholars, but also attract thousands of visitors from all over the world. An absorbing but probably unanswerable question remains: what exactly was the role of these far-sighted collectors in establishing (or even reinforcing) the consensus that now values so highly the works they selected? That the fact of a work's being acquired plays only a small part in the process is demonstrated by the collections themselves, since even the most apparently rigorously selected often include (sometimes in surprising numbers) works by mildly interesting artists consigned to obscurity and insignificant efforts by artists destined to remain unknown. That this is true of The Phillips Collection can be discovered only by studying its summary catalogue, although it seems plain that neither Duncan Phillips nor his wife had any illusions about these works. Rather, they both felt strongly that it was important to support and encourage the young and aspiring, and the not-so-young and needy.

Clearly, the adventurous collector plays – and has played – only one part in the complicated, sometimes vexed process that brings an artist to public attention in our present society, but it is an important role that acts as a hinge between personal preference and institutional support. Particularly in the first half of the twentieth century, in the absence of almost any kind of public support for new art, the role played by progressive American collectors was essential to what the sculptor Anthony Caro has called "the onward of art" in this country. By helping to insure that, at a crucial time in the history of modernism, the most innovative European art was seen here, often in the company of innovative American art, dedicated individuals such as John Quinn, the Cone sisters, Duncan Phillips, Robert H. Tannahill, and their colleagues offered an invaluable, stimulating challenge to artists and the audience for art alike. American visual culture would probably have developed very differently without their efforts.

Notes

1. The scope of this essay is deliberately limited. Only collectors who, like Robert H. Tannahill, acquired both European and American modernist art have been discussed, which has precluded examination of such important collectors as Gertrude Vanderbilt Whitney, Solomon R. Guggenheim, Roy R. Neuberger, William H. Lane, or Milton and Edith Lowenthal. Many interesting and significant collections, such as those of Ferdinand Howald or Walter and Louise Arensberg, among others, have been arbitrarily omitted because of space constraints. Ideally, the collecting activities of all of these individuals should be examined in detail, in the context of published art criticism of the time.

2. *Splendid Legacy: The Havemeyer Collection*, exhib. cat. by A.C. Frelinghuysen and G. Tinterow, New York, The Metropolitan Museum of Art, 1993.

3. Hugo van der Goes, *Portrait of a Man* (c. 1475, New York, Metropolitan Museum of Art), was purchased by the Havemeyers in 1904 as an Antonello da Messina; later scholarship has changed the attribution. Frelinghuysen and Tinterow, p. 343.

4. Quoted by Frelinghuysen and Tinterow, p. 235.

5. *Four Americans in Paris: The Collections of Gertrude Stein and Her Family*, exhib. cat., New York, Museum of Modern Art, 1970.

6. Leo Stein seems to have been the guiding force behind the purchase of many of the most adventurous works at the rue de Fleurus, before he lost interest in modernist art. Gertrude Stein's later, independent acquisitions were mainly mediocre Surrealist-derived works.

7. E.B. Hirschland, "The Cone Sisters and the Stein Family," in *Four Americans in Paris*, pp. 75–85; and *The Cone Collection*, (rev. edn. of *Handbook of the Cone Collection*, Baltimore, 1955), exhib. cat., Baltimore, Baltimore Museum of Art, 1970.

8. G. Boas, "The Cones," in *The Cone Collection*, p. 10.

9. *The Noble Buyer: John Quinn, Patron of the Avant-Garde*, exhib. cat. by J. Zilczer, Washington, D.C., Hirshhorn Museum and Sculpture Garden, Smithsonian Institution, 1978.

10. J.Q. to Marcel Duchamp, May 28, 1920. Zilczer, p. 45.

11. *Great French Paintings from the Barnes Foundation: Impressionist, Post-Impressionist, and Early Modern*, exhib. cat. by R.J. Wattenmaker and A. Distel, New York, Alfred A. Knopf, 1993.

12. Wattenmaker and Distel, p. 9.

13. Wattenmaker and Distel, p. 9.

14. *Duncan Phillips Centennial Exhibition*, exhib. cat., Washington, D.C., The Phillips Collection, 1986. E.D. Passantino (ed.), *The Phillips Collection: A Summary Catalogue*, Washington, D.C. (The Phillips Collection) 1985.

15. *Mad for Modernism: Earl Horter and his Collection*, exhib. cat. by I.H. Shoemaker, Philadelphia, Philadelphia Museum of Art, 1999.

16. M.L. Harth, "Robert Hudson Tannahill (1893–1969): Patron and Collector," diss., The University of Michigan, 1985. *The Robert Hudson Tannahill Bequest to The Detroit Institute of Arts*, exhib. cat., ed. G. Hood, Detroit, The Detroit Institute of Arts, 1970.

17. Halpert opened Our Gallery in Greenwich Village in 1926; the name was changed to The Downtown Gallery the following year. C. Troyen, "After Stieglitz: Edith Halpert and the Taste for Modern Art in America," in *The Lane Collection: 20th-Century Paintings in the American Tradition*, exhib. cat. by T.E. Stebbins Jr. and C. Troyen, Boston, Museum of Fine Arts, 1983, pp. 34–49.

18. Tannahill's purchases for The Detroit Institute of Arts were encyclopedic, ranging from antique American silver and furniture to Old Master works to international modernist paintings, sculpture, and graphics – and more.

19. J. Rewald, *The Paintings of Paul Cézanne: A Catalogue Raisonné*, New York (Harry N. Abrams) 1996, entry no. 507, pp. 338–42.

Paul Cézanne

(1839–1906)

Mont Sainte-Victoire, c. 1904–06

oil on canvas

55.6 × 46 cm

(21⅞ × 18⅛ in.)

THE DETROIT INSTITUTE OF ARTS

BEQUEST OF ROBERT H. TANNAHILL

Paul Cézanne

(1839–1906)

Mont Sainte-Victoire, 1886–87

oil on canvas

59.6 × 72.3 cm

(23½ × 28½ in.)

WASHINGTON, D.C.

THE PHILLIPS COLLECTION

Paul Cézanne

(1839–1906)

Fields at Bellevue, 1892–95

oil on canvas

36.1 × 50.1 cm

(14¼ × 19¾ in.)

WASHINGTON, D.C.

THE PHILLIPS COLLECTION

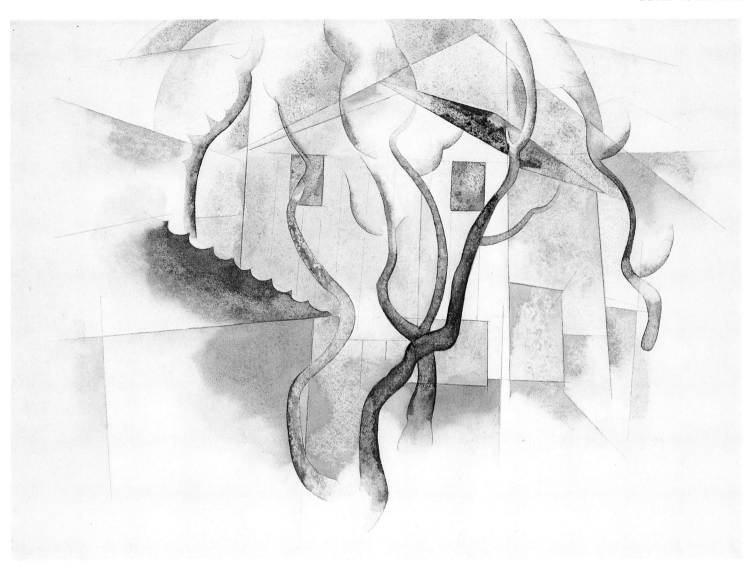

Charles Demuth
(1883–1935)
Trees and Barn, 1917
watercolor on wove paper
25.4 × 35.6 cm
(10 × 14 in.)
THE DETROIT INSTITUTE OF ARTS
BEQUEST OF ROBERT H. TANNAHILL

Charles Demuth

(1883–1935)

Red Chimneys, 1918

watercolor and graphite on

off-white wove paper

25.6 × 35.6 cm

(10⅛ × 14 in.)

Washington, D.C.

The Phillips Collection

Charles Demuth

(1883–1935)

Monument, Bermuda, 1917

watercolor on paper

35.5 × 25.4 cm

(14 × 10 in.)

WASHINGTON, D.C.

THE PHILLIPS COLLECTION

Lyonel Feininger
(1871–1956)
Sailboats, 1929
oil on canvas
43.2 × 72.4 cm
(17 × 28½ in.)
THE DETROIT INSTITUTE OF ARTS
GIFT OF ROBERT H. TANNAHILL

Lyonel Feininger
(1871–1956)
Village, 1927
oil on canvas
42.8 × 72.4 cm
(16⅞ × 28½ in.)
WASHINGTON, D.C.
THE PHILLIPS COLLECTION

Lyonel Feininger

(1871–1956)

Quimper, 1932

watercolor and black ink on

laid paper

29.8 × 46.7 cm

(12½ × 18 in.)

THE DETROIT INSTITUTE OF ARTS

BEQUEST OF ROBERT H. TANNAHILL

Lyonel Feininger

(1871–1956)

Waterfront, 1942

watercolor and black ink on

paper

29.2 × 45.7 cm

(11½ × 18 in.)

WASHINGTON, D.C.

THE PHILLIPS COLLECTION

George Grosz

(1893–1959)

New York Harbor, 1934

watercolor on off-white wove

paper

66.4 × 48.2 cm

(26⅛ × 19 in.)

THE DETROIT INSTITUTE OF ARTS

BEQUEST OF ROBERT H. TANNAHILL

George Grosz

(1893–1959)

Street in Harlem, 1916

watercolor on paper

62.2 × 43.1 cm

(24½ × 17 in.)

Washington, D.C.

The Phillips Collection

Paul Klee
(1879–1940)
Arrival of the Air Steamer,
1921
oil transfer and watercolor on
paper with laid texture,
mounted on thin cardboard
32.2 × 46 cm
(12¹¹⁄₁₆ × 18⅛ in.)
THE DETROIT INSTITUTE OF ARTS
BEQUEST OF ROBERT H. TANNAHILL

Paul Klee
(1879–1940)
Cathedral, 1924
watercolor and oil washes on
paper mounted on cardboard
and wood panel
30.1 × 35.5 cm
(11⅞ × 14 in.)
WASHINGTON, D.C.
THE PHILLIPS COLLECTION

Paul Klee

(1879–1940)

Tree Nursery, 1929

oil on canvas with incised

gesso ground

43.9 × 52.4 cm

(17¼ × 20⅝ in.)

WASHINGTON, D.C.

THE PHILLIPS COLLECTION

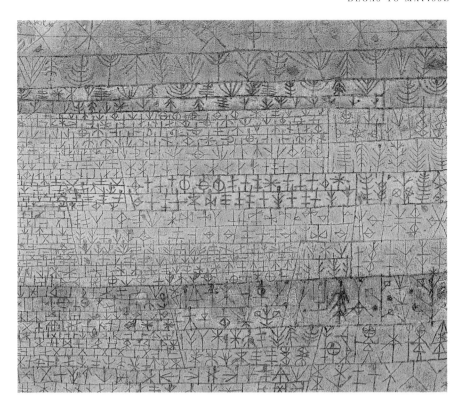

Paul Klee

(1879–1940)

Storm over the City, 1925

oil transfer and watercolor on

wove paper mounted on thin

cardboard; decorative lines in

black ink on support above

and below mounted sheet

38.4 × 41.9 cm

(15⅛ × 16½ in.)

THE DETROIT INSTITUTE OF ARTS

BEQUEST OF ROBERT H. TANNAHILL

Paul Klee

(1879–1940)

The Way to the Citadel, 1937

oil on canvas mounted on

cardboard

67 × 56.8 cm

(26⅜ × 22⅜ in.)

WASHINGTON, D.C.

THE PHILLIPS COLLECTION

Paul Klee

(1879–1940)

Garden, 1915

watercolor on paper mounted

on thin cardboard

13 × 24.1 cm

(5⅛ × 9½ in.)

THE DETROIT INSTITUTE OF ARTS

BEQUEST OF ROBERT H. TANNAHILL

Paul Klee

(1879–1940)

Garden Still Life, 1924

oil on paper mounted on

cardboard

33.6 × 22.8 cm

(13¼ × 9 in.) mount

28.5 × 19.6 cm

(11¼ × 7¾ in.) image

WASHINGTON, D.C.

THE PHILLIPS COLLECTION

Paul Klee

(1879–1940)

Botanical Laboratory, 1928

gouache, watercolor and ink

on paper mounted on

cardboard

39.3 × 27 cm

(15½ × 10⅝ in.) mount

31.4 × 23.4 cm

(12⅜ × 9¼ in.) image

WASHINGTON, D.C.

THE PHILLIPS COLLECTION

Henri Rousseau

(1844–1910)

Notre Dame, 1909

oil on canvas

32.7 × 40.9 cm

(12⅞ × 16⅛ in.)

WASHINGTON, D.C.

THE PHILLIPS COLLECTION

Henri Rousseau
(1844–1910)
The Environs of Paris, 1909
oil on canvas
46.4 × 55.6 cm
(18¼ × 21⅞ in.)
THE DETROIT INSTITUTE OF ARTS
BEQUEST OF ROBERT H. TANNAHILL

Karl Schmidt-Rottluff

(1884–1976)

Blossoming Trees, 1930–33

watercolor and brush and

black ink over black crayon

on white wove paper

50 × 70 cm

(20 × 27½ in.)

THE DETROIT INSTITUTE OF ARTS

BEQUEST OF ROBERT H. TANNAHILL

Georges Rouault

(1871–1958)

Tragic Landscape, 1930

ink and gouache on paper

47.6 × 59.6 cm

(18¾ × 23½ in.)

Washington, D.C.

The Phillips Collection

Collectors and Patrons

Robert Hudson Tannahill and Duncan Phillips:

Stephen Bennett Phillips

Collectors are often overlooked in the history of art. Without these philanthropists, the story of American museums would be a very different tale. Robert Hudson Tannahill (1893–1969) and Duncan Clinch Phillips (1886–1966) were two collectors who had a passion for modern art. Although they probably never met, they shared key connections in the art world, and their like-minded pursuit of modern art offers insights into personal choices and tastes in collecting during the first half of the twentieth century.

When Phillips decided to open his home as a museum in Washington, D.C., he merged his roles as patron and collector into one public entity. Tannahill, by contrast, kept his public and private sides distinct. First, he was a public patron of the arts through his generous support of The Detroit Institute of Arts, the Detroit Society of Arts and Crafts, and the Detroit Artists Market, all of which gave midwesterners exposure to styles and artists they may not otherwise have seen. Second, he was a private collector, who allowed only a few invited guests to view his collection of modern art in his home. Though their stories are different, Phillips and Tannahill pursued the same goal – to educate the public about modern art.

Phillips's and Tannahill's adventurous artistic vision was no accident, but rather a product of their backgrounds.

Paul Gauguin

Self-Portrait, c. 1893

(DETAIL; SEE PAGE 76)

Born into affluent, established families and educated at
Ivy League schools, they shared an approach to
collecting that had nothing to do with status or prestige.
Theirs was a philanthropic approach, fostered, in part,
by their secure social station.

The Formative Years

Though Phillips was seven years older than Tannahill,
both men were raised in similar backgrounds in late
nineteenth-century America. They were both born in
industrial cities – Phillips in Pittsburgh and Tannahill in
Detroit – and both of their maternal families had
significant wealth. Phillips's maternal grandfather,
James Laughlin, was a banker and co-founder of the Jones
and Laughlin Steel Company, and his father founded a
company that manufactured glass.[2] Tannahill's maternal
family founded the J.L. Hudson department store, where
his father was vice-president. Tannahill became further
entwined with one of America's great industrialist
families when his first cousin, Eleanor Clay, married
Edsel Ford, son of Henry Ford, the automobile magnate.[3]

Given their privileged backgrounds, both men were free
to pursue interests without regard to earning a living. In
the first two decades of this century, Phillips saw himself
as a writer and an art critic. During his undergraduate
years at Yale University, he wrote twelve articles for the
Yale Literary Magazine and was elected editor in his
senior year. After graduating from Yale in 1908, his art
reviews were published in such prominent magazines as
Scribner's Magazine, Art and Progress, and the
International Studio. In 1914, he published his first book,
*The Enchantment of Art as Part of the Enchantment of
Experience*, a compilation of seventeen essays.[4]

Tannahill also considered himself a writer, though of an
entirely different nature. After receiving a Master of
Arts degree from Harvard University in 1916, he worked
toward becoming a playwright. In the early 1920s, he
wrote four plays and even had two copyrighted, though
none was produced. While he did not make a living as a
writer, he considered it his occupation throughout the
1920s.[5]

At an early age, both Phillips and Tannahill became
interested in collecting. Although their parents were not
collectors, Duncan and his older brother, James, started
acquiring art after college. In 1912, Duncan used part of
his New York City living allowance to buy *High
Bridge–Early Moon* (by 1910) by Ernest Lawson. When,
in 1916, the brothers asked their parents to provide them
with a fund to purchase art, their parents agreed to give
them an annual stipend of $10,000.[6]

As an only child, Tannahill was first exposed to
collecting through his mother, who was an early collector
of American decorative arts. At the age of ten, he
accompanied her on one of her many buying trips to the
East Coast. This probably instilled in him an interest in
collecting and definitely led to a lifelong appreciation of
the decorative arts. Not surprisingly, his early collecting
focused on the decorative arts. The first works to enter
his collection were a group of etchings of English
monarchs. Not until the 1930s would he begin
aggressively to buy works by modern artists. Though he
was at least a decade behind collectors of modern art in
the East, Tannahill was one of the earliest and most
significant collectors in Detroit in the 1930s and 1940s.[7]
Even though Phillips and Tannahill were educated at
Ivy League universities, they both developed their sense
of connoisseurship through independent study and

travel. In 1910 the Phillips family traveled to Japan and China, which was an ambitious trip for that time. Over the next two years, Phillips made two trips to Europe, where he visited the great museums and studied many of their paintings. On his second trip he visited the noted French art dealer Paul Durand-Ruel, who would serve him well as he began actively to buy French art in the 1920s.[8] About this same time, Tannahill also took the first of many trips to Europe. He spent most of his time in France, where he developed an abiding love for the country's art, language, and culture.[9]

Collecting and the Armory Show

Phillips and Tannahill did not buy major works of art when they were in France in the second decade of the twentieth century. Modernism had yet to take hold of their vision. In fact, they were a decade behind other American collectors who were actively acquiring works from the School of Paris. But once they developed an eye for modern art, they began to forge collections that few of their contemporaries could match in quality and scope.

As early as 1905, a few collectors such as the American expatriates Gertrude and Leo Stein, were buying works by Paul Cézanne, Henri Matisse, and Pablo Picasso.[10] A few years later, other Americans such as Albert Barnes and Henry and Louisine Havemeyer were buying paintings by Cézanne, among others, at French auctions and from the galleries of such well-known Paris dealers as Durand-Ruel, Bernheim-Jeune, Vollard, and Druet.[11] The Armory Show, which opened in New York in 1913 and traveled to Chicago and Boston, was an important event in the history of collecting because it introduced

many collectors to modern art, prompting many of them to reconsider their conservative taste.[12] In the end, the New York lawyer John Quinn, the exhibition's legal adviser as well as a collector of Cézanne, Vincent van Gogh, and Paul Gauguin, purchased the largest number of works from the show. After Quinn, the most enthusiastic collector at the Armory Show was the Chicago lawyer Arthur Jerome Eddy, who bought eighteen paintings and seven lithographs. Walter Arensberg, Albert Barnes, Stephen Clark, Katherine Dreier, Hamilton Easter Field, A.E. Gallatin, and Edward Root also purchased works from the exhibition, becoming avid collectors of modern art. Arensberg wanted to purchase a work on paper by Auguste Rodin but hesitated and lost it to William R. Valentiner, a young curator at the Metropolitan, who would go on to become the director of The Detroit Institute of Arts and a friend and adviser to Tannahill.[13]

The Armory Show also cultivated an appreciation of modern art in the collector Lillie Bliss, who would indirectly have a similar effect on Phillips and Tannahill. The artist Arthur B. Davies, her adviser and one of the show's organizers, would later become a friend of Phillips; indeed, Davies is credited with helping Phillips understand modernism. Davies advised Bliss to begin her collection of modern art by making purchases at the Armory Show. She bought an oil and a pastel by Odilon Redon as well as eighteen works on paper by such artists as Cézanne, Gauguin, and Pierre-Auguste Renoir. These were not daring acquisitions, but they showed her willingness to accept more radical works of art. Over the next few decades, Bliss put together an exemplary collection of modern art, which became a major component of the Museum of Modern Art (MoMA) in New York.[14] In 1936, MoMA would loan

The Phillips residence at
1600 21ˢᵗ Street, c. 1900

the Bliss collection to the Detroit Committee of the Museum of Modern Art, New York, which Tannahill helped to establish.[15]

Phillips attended the Armory Show but was not prepared to embrace the startling work he saw there. He wrote a review for the *International Studio* that was critical of the exhibition and many of the modern artists whose works he would collect a decade or two later.[16] Whether Tannahill attended the Armory Show is not known, but it is doubtful that he would have made the effort, given his focus on American decorative arts as a young man.

Phillips was not alone in his hesitation about modern art at the time of the Armory Show. Many collectors were still not ready for the more avant-garde works that they saw in the exhibition. Barnes, who was by then a serious collector, purchased only one work from the exhibition, passing up reasonably priced works by such important artists as Matisse, whose paintings he would later passionately collect. With her purchase of lithographs by Gauguin and Redon, Dreier indicated her reluctance to embrace the radical side of modernism that she later went on to support. Arensberg bought a few minor works from the exhibition before it closed at its third venue but expressed his regret at not having purchased more daring pieces. Afterwards, he made a

concerted effort to find the works he had failed to buy the first time.[17]

The enthusiasm for modernism that followed the Armory Show demonstrated that Old Master paintings were no longer the only works that collectors wanted to buy.[18] Although dealers such as Durand-Ruel, Knoedler, and Wildenstein had galleries in New York, only a fledgling art market existed in the city in the late nineteenth and early twentieth centuries because American collectors usually traveled to Europe to buy works.[19] After 1910, more collectors emerged who were interested in buying contemporary art. Their enthusiasm was nurtured, in part, by the repeal of the Tariff Act in 1913, which had imposed a duty on imported artworks produced within the past twenty years.[20] Dealers responded to this new demand by opening modern art galleries in New York.[21] This collecting fervor gained momentum with the prosperity of the 1920s. As the demand for works increased, prices for quality works rose ever higher, and many undiscriminating collectors were willing to pay high prices for mediocre works of art.[22] Having an eye for quality was critical, and Phillips and Tannahill could both claim this talent.

Marjorie and Duncan Phillips in the Main Gallery of what was then called The Phillips Memorial Art Gallery, *c.* 1922. Photograph by Clara E. Sipprel.

The Early Years

Although Phillips and Tannahill demonstrated an interest in art early on, they did not begin collecting seriously until they became financially comfortable. In 1917–18, when Phillips was in his early thirties, his father and brother died, providing him with an inheritance and a strong desire to collect art and to open a museum in their memory.[23] Tannahill's mother died in 1921, followed by his father four years later. Both parents left their entire estate to their only child, who was in his early thirties, thus providing Tannahill with enough money to secure him financially security even during the economic downturn of the 1930s.[24]

With financial resources in hand, Phillips and Tannahill began buying works of art. Phillips collected at a more frenzied pace to realize his ambition to open a public museum of modern art in memory of his father and brother. Between 1918 and 1921, the year the collection opened to the public, he purchased more than two hundred paintings and added a second-floor gallery on to his family's home in Washington, D.C.[25]

Tannahill began his sustained buying period only in the 1930s. During the 1920s he acquired only one modern work, a watercolor by the German Expressionist Emil Nolde. Yet this purchase signaled Tannahill's willingness to run counter to the conservative tastes of other collectors in Detroit as he developed his personal collecting style. He would embrace this avant-garde spirit more fully in the 1930s, though, like Phillips, his taste would never stray too far from his genteel background to be considered radical.[26]

In the 1920s, Phillips was busy collecting work and planning shows for his new museum. Throughout the decade, he purchased more than 350 works of art, among them *The Luncheon of the Boating Party* (1880–81; see illus., p. 21), one of Renoir's masterworks. Other European acquisitions included works by Cézanne, Picasso, Honoré Daumier, El Greco, Pierre Bonnard, Georges Braque, and Edouard Manet. Phillips's interest in American modernists emerged as early as 1921, when he bought a painting by Marsden Hartley. His acquisition in 1926 of works by Arthur Dove and Georgia O'Keeffe was the first of paintings by these artists for a museum collection. Other American artists whose art Phillips collected included Albert Pinkham Ryder, Charles Demuth, Edward Hopper, and John Marin.[27] As his collection grew, he put together more than thirty-five installations, which were culled from his collection or borrowed from artists, dealers, or other museums.[28]

During the same decade, Tannahill was becoming involved with his hometown museum, The Detroit Institute of Arts. His involvement probably dates to 1919, when his mother loaned the museum some objects from her American decorative arts collection. In 1926, he followed her example and gave the museum two pieces of decorative art as his first donation. That same year, his article on early American furniture was published in the *Bulletin*, the museum's publication. Tannahill's expertise in the decorative arts was acknowledged in 1927 when The Detroit Institute of Arts made him an honorary curator of American art.[29]

Tannahill's involvement with the museum increased in the 1920s after the arrival of its charismatic director, William R. Valentiner, a seasoned museum professional, later credited with transforming The Detroit Institute of Arts from a small art gallery into one of the great museums in the country.[30] While Phillips and Valentiner were both intent on promoting their institutions' growth, they differed in the means they used to achieve that goal. Because he and his museum were synonymous, Phillips could find a work he wanted for his collection and buy it without having to gain committee approval or find a wealthy donor. Valentiner, understanding that a museum needed to cultivate collectors and advise them on their purchases in order to develop a first-rate collection through bequests, began the task of cultivating local collectors. While he admired members of the older generation of Detroit society such as Henry Ford, he realized that the greatest potential asset of The Detroit Institute of Arts lay in the next generation of young collectors, such as Edsel Ford and Robert Tannahill. Around 1925, Valentiner started teaching private art history classes to members of the Ford and Kanzler families, both related by marriage to Tannahill. At times

Valentiner even accompanied the Fords on trips abroad and helped steer their purchases of art. Fortunately, Tannahill was already knowledgeable about art, so Valentiner had to spend less time instructing him, thus allowing them to develop a true friendship. Valentiner's advice notwithstanding, Tannahill often based his final purchases on his own innate aesthetic judgment. One area of exception was German art, about which Valentiner had deep knowledge and enthusiasm.[31]

The Depression Years

The economic contraction of the early 1930s forced many collectors to cut back on their purchases. Fortunately, by the mid-1930s, the high prices and speculative purchases of the 1920s gave way to more realistic valuations and a return to quality. General collecting tastes were shifting away from the Old Masters and English portraiture toward Impressionist, Post-Impressionist, and contemporary art.[32] Despite the depressed economy, Tannahill began his most active collecting in this climate.[33] Phillips was similarly undaunted.

The year of Wall Street's collapse, Phillips was elected to MoMA's Board of Trustees. In 1930, Phillips demonstrated his commitment to educate the public about modern art by moving his family offsite and expanding his museum from two galleries to virtually his entire former residence. Relocating his home provided space for temporary exhibitions and more galleries in which to display his growing collection.[34] Phillips's zeal for collecting, however, was affected by the Depression: his pace slowed in 1932 and did not pick up again until 1937. During this five-year period he bought works mainly by

Robert Hudson Tannahill
and Diego Rivera, 1932.

contemporary American artists, whom he was committed to supporting.[35] In the fall of 1932, Phillips was forced to close the Phillips Gallery Art School for a year, one year after he had opened it, and to limit the museum's visiting hours to Saturdays. He also sent some of his paintings on tour to help raise funds.[36] Between 1933 and 1936, however, he spent extravagantly on one European masterwork each year – Georges Rouault's *Circus Trio* (1924), Braque's *Round Table* (1929), Bonnard's *Terrace* (1918), and Francisco de Goya's *Repentant Peter* (c. 1820–24), respectively.[37]

For Tannahill, the 1930s were arguably the most important years in his life as a collector and patron of the arts. He became more involved with The Detroit Institute of Arts, first as a trustee, then as a member of its Arts Commission. He chaired a group called the Friends of Modern Art, which sought to build a collection of modern art at The Detroit Institute of Arts by donating at least one work per year.[38] Together with Edsel Ford, Tannahill funded Diego Rivera's stay in Detroit in 1932, during which time Rivera created a series of murals at The Detroit Institute of Art.[39] That same year, he co-founded the Young Artists Market to help support local artists. In 1935, he expanded his involvement in contemporary art by helping to create the Detroit Committee of the Museum of Modern Art, dedicated to promoting interest in modern art in areas other than New York.[40]

Between 1930 and 1939, Tannahill acquired sixty-four works of art, more than double the number of works he bought for his collection over the next decade. Tannahill may well have been influenced by MoMA, which was beginning to assert its dominance in modern art. Interesting similarities are apparent between Tannahill's

collection and the works in the Bliss collection, bequeathed to MoMA in 1931 and displayed in Detroit in 1936.[41] The works Tannahill purchased in the 1930s are often considered his most important. More than half of these acquisitions are paintings, most of which are French. Tannahill's taste was often more advanced than his fellow collectors in Detroit. Proposing an acquisition from the Friends of Modern Art to The Detroit Institute of Arts, Tannahill wrote in 1932, "I was afraid that some of the more conservative members wouldn't like it, that they would pick something more easily understood."[42]

Before The Detroit Institute of Arts started exhibiting contemporary art, Tannahill convinced the Detroit Society of Arts and Crafts in 1931 to open gallery space to exhibit modern art – one of his most significant contributions to the city's cultural life. In promoting the idea, Tannahill wrote:

Detroit has lagged far behind eastern cities in the opportunities it has provided to see the best of modern art. The almost unparalleled success of the Modern Museum in New York City, the thousands of persons who viewed its exhibitions … seem to prove beyond a doubt that there is a large public interested in contemporary art. Thus we feel there is a definite need in Detroit for a gallery where thoughtfully chosen examples of contemporary sculpture, prints, and paintings may be shown.[43]

In creating a respectable gallery space out of a salesroom in the Detroit Society of Arts and Crafts building, Tannahill tried to accomplish many of the same goals in Detroit that Phillips was achieving in Washington, D.C. He often headed the exhibition committee, organized major loan shows, and, like Phillips, sometimes paid their expenses.[44]

Marsden Hartley

(1877–1943)

Log Jam, Penobscot Bay,

1940–41

oil on canvas

76.4 × 104 cm

(30 × 40⅞ in.)

The Detroit Institute of Arts

Gift of Robert H. Tannahill

Though no documentation exists to prove that Tannahill and Phillips knew of each other during Tannahill's involvement with the society's modern art gallery, their mutual connections in New York suggest that they did. It is likely that Tannahill knew about Phillips through publicity surrounding his museum and through books and articles Phillips had written on art. They certainly knew many of the same people. Edith Halpert, the New York dealer best known for her Downtown Gallery, was a friend of Phillips and Tannahill and may have been a conduit between them. Halpert advised Tannahill about many of his exhibitions of American art and sold works by many of the same artists to both collectors.[45] Moreover, Valentiner knew about Phillips and most likely told Tannahill about him. In late 1943, Valentiner

visited The Phillips Collection to see a loan show of twenty-nine paintings by Hartley, including the painting *Log Jam, Penobscot Bay* (1940–41), which he convinced Tannahill to buy and give to The Detroit Institute of Arts. Given such close connections, it would be hard to believe that the two men did not know about each other. Tannahill's involvement with such modern art organizations as MoMA as well as such New York dealers as Alfred Stieglitz would surely have made him aware of the activities of other collectors of modern art.[46]

Marsden Hartley

(1877–1943)

Wood Lot, Maine Woods, 1939

oil on canvas

71.4 × 55.8 cm

(28½ × 22 in.)

WASHINGTON, D.C.

THE PHILLIPS COLLECTION

Modern Art in the Midwest

During its existence from 1932 to 1941, the modern art gallery at the Detroit Society of Arts and Crafts held fifty exhibitions, many of which presented nineteenth- and twentieth-century European and American art.[47] For his exhibition program, Tannahill traced modern art to Impressionism, unlike MoMA, which presented Post-Impressionism as the beginning of modernism. Exhibitions ranged from one- and two-person exhibitions to more diverse group shows, which were usually organized around the holdings of New York galleries with additions from Detroit collections, including Tannahill's. The gallery also exhibited works from such private collections as the Ambroise Vollard collection and the Lillie P. Bliss collection, by this time

part of MoMA. In fact, Tannahill tried to create an exhibition program for the gallery that was geared toward collectors, often offering artworks for sale at reasonable prices. Tannahill's numerous purchases from the exhibitions helped form the foundation for his private collection as well as enhance that of The Detroit Institute of Arts.[48]

Some of the most important exhibitions at the society's modern art gallery included American art. Tannahill opened the gallery in 1932 with an exhibition of American folk art, one of the first shows in the country to focus on the formal similarities between American folk art and contemporary art.[49] For the exhibition *American Contemporary Painting and Sculpture* that same year, Tannahill and Halpert brought together fifty-seven works by such artists as Hartley, Marin, O'Keeffe, Demuth, Charles Burchfield, Stuart Davis, and Charles Sheeler. Many of these artists were later invited to have one- or two-person exhibitions at the gallery. One such show, in 1934, featured the work of Marin and O'Keeffe, the first major exhibition of their work in the Midwest.[50]

Equally impressive were the group shows Tannahill and Valentiner organized of contemporary French artists, including Renoir, Cézanne, Degas, Gauguin, Amedeo Modigliani, and Henri Rousseau. Tannahill considered the gallery's exhibition of works by Rouault and Matisse in 1934 to be one of the best in Detroit.[51] Six years later, Tannahill put together an exhibition of drawings and watercolors by Picasso. Tannahill was an early collector of Picasso's work in this country, an interest that may have been stimulated by MoMA's exhibition *Painting in Paris* in 1930.[52]

Valentiner's enthusiasm for contemporary German art insured its inclusion in the modern art gallery's exhibition program. The most significant of these exhibitions was held in 1937 in response to *Degenerate Art*, the Nazi-sponsored exhibition designed to discredit modern art. Having seen the Munich exhibition of works confiscated by the Nazis, Valentiner and Tannahill were outraged enough to mount a provocative exhibition of works from Detroit collections by some of the same artists. Other noteworthy shows included a memorial exhibition for Paul Klee in 1940, but the Detroit public was not ready for Klee's work, resulting in its poor reception.[53]

As one of the earliest collectors of African art in this country, Tannahill understood its influence on many modern artists and wanted to demonstrate this relationship in his collection and exhibitions. To coincide with the exhibition of works from the Bliss collection at the society's modern art gallery, Tannahill organized an exhibition of African art from the Pierre Matisse Gallery in New York. This exhibition was not only the first of its kind in Detroit, but also one of the first in the country, occurring only a year after MoMA's ground-breaking exhibition of African art in 1935.[54]

Unfortunately, the modern art gallery had to close in 1941 when the United States entered the Second World War. During its run, the gallery successfully introduced modern art to Detroit and the Midwest, often broadening its visitors' aesthetic sensibilities. While many people helped with the gallery, Tannahill was the driving force behind its nine-year existence, organizing exhibitions that were important as well as innovative.[55]

A Broad View of Modernism

During the time of the society's modern art gallery, Phillips was pursuing many of the same goals but on a larger scale. He held some 135 exhibitions at his museum. Phillips took a broader view of modernism than Tannahill or MoMA, tracing its sources back to Egyptian art and up through Giorgione, El Greco, Goya, and into the twentieth century. Often the exhibitions were drawn from his permanent collection, but the museum was also the venue for loan exhibitions and shows of work by students at the art school.[56]

After Phillips opened up the first two floors of his house to the museum, he featured more one-person exhibitions by Marin, Dove, Burchfield, Walt Kuhn, Harold Weston, Gifford Beal, Louis Eilshemius, Constantin Guys, Henri de Toulouse-Lautrec, and Edouard Vuillard, among others. Unlike Tannahill, Phillips had to scale back his exhibition program in the mid-1930s. To help local artists during this tough economic time, in 1935 Phillips held the first of what would become an annual group exhibition of work by artists from Washington, D.C. By 1937, his exhibition schedule had returned to its double-digit pace. Phillips held an exhibition of watercolors and oils by Klee in 1938, the same year he organized the exhibition *Picasso and Marin*, demonstrating his preference for showing American and European artists side by side.[57]

Henri Rousseau
(1844–1910)
Vase of Flowers,
19th–20th century
oil on canvas
33.3 × 24.1 cm
(13⅛ × 9½ in.)
The Detroit Institute of Arts
Bequest of Robert H. Tannahill

Main Gallery of The Phillips Collection, 1927. Pictures on the facing wall include Paul Cézanne's *Mont Sainte-Victoire*.

Annex gallery at The Phillips Collection, 1960, with pictures by Henri Matisse, El Greco, and Jean-Baptiste-Camille Corot.

The Final Decades

Phillips's acquisitions reached a peak in the 1940s, when he purchased more than five hundred works of art for the museum.[58] Though his pace of collecting declined in the 1950s, his exhibition schedule became more ambitious. He organized larger loan shows and showed important exhibitions arranged by other arts organizations.[59]

In 1960, Phillips opened a long-awaited addition to the museum called the Annex (known today as the Goh Annex). It provided additional space for special exhibitions and to display the permanent collection, including an outdoor sculpture courtyard. One of the highlights of the new building was a small room designated for Mark Rothko's painting. This was the first public room in America where visitors could see Rothko's paintings the way the artist wanted them viewed – by themselves, without the distraction of works by other artists.[60] When Phillips died in 1966, he left the museum a small endowment, 1800 works of art, and the imperative that the collection continue to grow. "It must be kept vital," he wrote, "as it always has been, as a place for enlightenment, for enjoyment, for discovery, by frequent rearrangements of the collection and for the enrichments of new acquisitions."[61]

The early 1940s were not happy years in Tannahill's life. He suffered a period of illness that made him withdraw socially and restrict his involvement in the arts. During this time he lost several individuals who were important in his life. Edsel Ford, to whom he was especially close through his first cousin, Eleanor Clay Ford, died unexpectedly in 1943, followed the next year by his aunt, Eliza Clay, with whom he had lived since the early 1920s.[62] But probably the biggest blow to Tannahill occurred in 1945, when his close friend Valentiner retired from The Detroit Institute of Arts and moved away from the city.[63]

Tannahill renewed his involvement with local arts organizations and his support of local artists in the mid-1940s. Partly through his financial support, The Detroit Institute of Arts was able to purchase works by Michigan artists for its collection. These works were the focus of Tannahill's exhibition *Abstract Art Is Reality* in 1952, designed to educate viewers about abstraction. He also continued his involvement with the Artists Market.[64]

Perhaps the the most significant event for Tannahill during this period was his new house in Grosse Point, which overlooked Lake St. Claire. Like Phillips, Tannahill was an unpretentious man, and his new house

Interior views of Robert Hudson Tannahill's residence,
October 1969.

reflected this. The two-story home had a modern feeling, conveyed by its simple lines and sparse architectural detailing. The interior was deliberately understated and expansive to highlight Tannahill's collection of painting and sculpture.[65] Tannahill insisted on subdued colors for the fabrics and off-white tones for the walls. He installed his treasured French works in the most public rooms on the first floor. The American and German works occupied the second floor, and the African pieces were displayed in the second-floor study.[66]

During the 1940s, Tannahill purchased a few important works by European artists but only two works by American artists – Winslow Homer and Morris Graves – for his private collection. By the 1950s and 1960s, he had begun to slow down markedly in his personal collecting, and was concentrating on buying for The Detroit Institute of Arts. Among the important works added to his personal collection during these years were *Woman with a Headband* by Degas and drawings by Käthe Kollwitz. Tannahill now seemed more attracted to sculpture and purchased works by Rodin, Matisse, and Degas. African art continued to hold its appeal during his last few years.[67] In the end, Valentiner believed that Tannahill had amassed one of the greatest collections of modern art in the Midwest.[68]

Tannahill was generous in his gifts of art to The Detroit Institute of Arts in the 1940s, 1950s, and 1960s. During the 1940s, he gave more than two hundred objects, many of them in memory of his aunt. Of the 468 objects he gave to the museum before his death, many were purchased expressly for it.[69] In appreciation of his almost thirty-year service on the institute's Arts Commission, the board stated that "no individual has been more intimately connected, and for a longer time, with the Art Museum of our City and few have had its growth so much at heart as Mr. Tannahill." The article in the *Detroit News* that reported the board's resolution even went as far as to estimate the value of his gifts to the museum at more than $300,000. Because Tannahill had avoided publicity throughout his life, he probably considered such published accounts highly invasive of his privacy. Yet his generosity was not to go unnoticed. In 1966 The Detroit Institute of Arts named its American galleries the Robert Hudson Tannahill Wing of American Art.[70]

When Tannahill died in 1969, he left The Detroit Institute of Arts almost all of his property and his entire private art collection of more than four hundred objects. The paintings, including French works dating from 1873 to 1923, were the most important component of his collection, which included sculpture, drawings and other

Käthe Kollwitz

(1867–1945)

Head of a Woman, n.d.

aquatint and etching, 19/50

52.7 × 39.3 cm

(20¾ × 15½ in.) sheet

34.9 × 31.7 cm

(13¾ × 12½ in.) image

WASHINGTON, D.C.

THE PHILLIPS COLLECTION

GIFT OF DWIGHT CLARK, *c.* 1934

works on paper, and African objects. Of the works on paper, forty were by American artists, with Marin and Demuth responsible for the largest group. Almost all of Tannahill's forty-nine sculptures were small, dark European bronzes from the late nineteenth or early twentieth century.[71]

In addition to his collection, Tannahill left The Detroit Institute of Arts fifty percent of the income from the Robert Hudson Tannahill Foundation, to be used for new acquisitions. One-third was to be applied toward the purchase of impressionistic art, another third for the acquisition of American colonial and federal objects, and the final third for artwork produced before 1925.[72]

Choices over a Lifetime

In comparing the choices made by Duncan Phillips and Robert Tannahill, one can find similarities and differences in the collections they formed. Neither collector sought to create an encyclopedic collection or to represent fully the modern art movement. Instead, they chose works that could carry on a dialogue through their formal qualities of line, shape, and color. Tannahill was drawn more to portraits and figures, often nude, while Phillips was generally attracted to landscapes and interiors. Formally, Tannahill's choices focused more on line and form than color and tended toward classical simplicity, contemplation, restraint, and melancholy. Sensuousness is rare in his collection.[73] By contrast, Phillips was a romantic with an intense response to color. Celebrating the vibrancy of Matisse's work, he focused as much on the artist's palette as on his use of line: "Now I am ready to recognize in Matisse a daring and lucid agitator for direct decorative expression and luminous chromatic experiment."[74]

Though both Tannahill and Phillips collected American art, the French paintings in their collections – more so for Tannahill than for Phillips – are the works that are

Käthe Kollwitz

(1867–1945)

Burial, c. 1903

charcoal and pastel with

touches of white chalk on

light-brown cardboard or

composition board

54.7 × 47.9 cm

(16 × 14 in.)

The Detroit Institute of Arts

Bequest of Robert H. Tannahill

considered the greatest by art historians.[75] Of the School of Paris artists, Cézanne appealed to both collectors. Overall, Tannahill and Phillips were conservative in their choices of Picasso's work, preferring paintings done in the first quarter of the twentieth century, when Picasso was classical and melancholy in his depiction of human forms.[76] Among twentieth-century French artists, both Phillips and Tannahill collected Braque, Rouault, and Chaim Soutine. While Phillips had a great enthusiasm for Bonnard and actively collected Raoul Dufy, Tannahill showed no interest in either artist.

Because of Valentiner's knowledge of and enthusiasm for German modernist art, Tannahill was ahead of Phillips in this realm.[77] Both collectors had a passion for Klee's work at a time when few other collectors were interested in the artist. MoMA's retrospective in 1930 probably familiarized them with Klee's work.[78] Phillips's collection of twentieth-century German works was not fleshed out until the early 1950s, when the collector

Katherine S. Dreier died and left part of her private collection to Phillips.[79]

Despite Tannahill's great love of modern art, it did not extend to non-representational art. He eschewed work whose pictorial reference was not readily grounded in the real world. Though he had the opportunity to collect abstract work by such artists as Wassily Kandinsky, Joan Miró, Piet Mondrian, Willem de Kooning, and Jackson Pollock in the 1940s and 1950s, he chose not to do so. For this reason, his role as a proponent of modernism in Detroit was superseded by younger collectors who took a more active role in promoting abstract painting.[80] Although Phillips was more receptive to non-representational art, in many cases he chose to purchase only a single work representative of each artist's œuvre.[81]

Over his lifetime, Phillips directed his collecting energy toward his public museum; his private collection was secondary in nature. In contrast, Tannahill had two

Morris Graves

(born 1910)

Wounded Gull, 20th century

watercolor and gouache on

paper

67.3 × 77.2 cm

(26½ × 28⅜ in.)

THE DETROIT INSTITUTE OF ARTS

BEQUEST OF ROBERT H. TANNAHILL

important collections – his private collection and his public collection. Though Tannahill enjoyed buying works for The Detroit Institute of Art, he was very guarded about his private collection. He did not like to loan works from his private collection and opted to remain anonymous when he did. Only once, for an exhibition at The Detroit Institute of Arts in 1932, did Tannahill allow his name to be associated with his collection.[82]

In the end, Phillips and Tannahill defy easy categorization. They were both very private men who were committed to enriching the public's understanding of modern art. They both bought works they found visually stimulating without trying to put together a collection that was comprehensive or socially acceptable. Perry Rathbone noted that the personal nature of Tannahill's collection "was very unlike that of the typical rich man at the time."[83] The same could be said about Phillips. By buying works they liked, Phillips and Tannahill often chose pieces that were not universally sanctioned by their social peers. But time has validated their choices, as yesterday's avant-garde works of art become today's accepted masterworks.

Morris Graves

(born 1910)

Wounded Gull, 1943

gouache on paper

67.6 × 76.8 cm

(26⅝ × 30¼ in.)

WASHINGTON, D.C.

THE PHILLIPS COLLECTION

Notes

This essay is indebted to Marjorie Leslie Harth's extensive research on Robert Hudson Tannahill.

1. Marjorie Leslie Harth, "Robert Hudson Tannahill (1893–1969): Patron and Collector," diss., University of Michigan, 1985, pp. 106, 161–62.

2. Erika D. Passantino and Sarah Martin, "Chronology," in *Duncan Phillips: Centennial Exhibition*, exhib. cat.,Washington, D.C., The Phillips Collection, 1986, p. 26.

3. Harth, p. 21.

4. Duncan Phillips, *The Enchantment of Art as Part of the Enchantment of Experience: Fifteen Years Later*, 2nd edn., rev., Washington, D.C. (Phillips Publications) 1927; Passantino and Martin, pp. 26–28; Maura K. Parrott, "Duncan Phillips: Life and Writings – A Chronology," Washington, D.C. (The Phillips Collection) n.p.

5. For his 1927 passport, Tannahill listed his occupation as "playwright." Harth, pp. 22–24.

6. Passantino and Martin, p. 28; Parrott, "Phillips: Life and Writings," n.p.

7. Harth, pp. 21–25, 153. Other collectors of modernist work in Detroit were Lillian Henkel Haass, the Kampermans, and John S. Newberry. Next to Tannahill, Newberry was Detroit's most important collector of modern art. Newberry's collection contains mostly works on paper; see Harth, pp. 153–55.

8. Passantino and Martin, p. 27; Parrott, "Phillips: Life and Writings," n.p.

9. Harth, p. 22.

10. Anne Distel, "Dr. Barnes in Paris," in *Great French Paintings from the Barnes Foundation: Impressionist, Post-Impressionist and Early Modern*, exhib. cat. by R.J. Wattenmaker and A. Distel, New York, Alfred A. Knopf, 1993, p. 33.

11. *Ibid.*, pp. 29–33.

12. Milton W. Brown, *The Story of the Armory Show*, New York (Abbeville Press) 1988, pp. 119–20, 131.

13. *Ibid.*, pp. 119–29.

14. *Ibid.*, pp. 121.

15. Mary Jane Jacob, "The Modern Art Gallery 1932–1941," in *Arts and Crafts in Detroit 1906–1976: The Movement, the Society, the School*, exhib. cat., Detroit, The Detroit Institute of Arts, 1977, p. 166. The Detroit Committee of the Museum of Modern Art held the exhibition of the Bliss collection at the Detroit Society of Arts and Crafts's modern art gallery.

16. Duncan Phillips, "Revolutions and Reactions in Painting," *International Studio*, 51, December 1913, pp. cxxiii–cxxix.

17. Brown, pp. 127–31.

18. *Ibid.*, pp. 131–32.

19. Germain Seligman, *Merchants of Art: 1880–1960*, New York (Appleton Century-Crofts) 1961, pp. 18–19.

20. Harth, pp. 5–6.

21. Brown, pp. 131–32.

22. Seligman, p. 177.

23. Passantino and Martin, p. 29.

24. Harth, p. 23.

25. Passantino and Martin, p. 29.

26. Harth, pp. 25–26.

27. Maura K. Parrott and Research Office staff, "Chronology of Acquisitions," Washington, D.C. (The Phillips Collection) 1989, n.p.

28. "Exhibitions at The Phillips Collection," Appendix A in Erika D. Passantino (ed.), *The Eye of Duncan Phillips: A Collection in the Making*, New Haven, CT (The Phillips Collection in association with Yale University Press) 1999, pp. 659–74.

29. Harth, pp. 23–24, 26.

30. *Ibid.*, pp. 26, 79; Margaret Sterne, *The Passionate Eye: The Life of Dr. William R. Valentiner*, Detroit (Wayne State University Press) 1980, pp. 299–303.

31. Harth, pp. 28–36.

32. Seligman, pp. 177–78.

33. Harth, p. 43.

34. Passantino and Martin, p. 36; Parrott, "Phillips: Life and Writings," n.p.

35. These American artists included Hartley, Dove, Marin, Harold Weston, Stuart Davis, Charles Burchfield, Augustus Vincent Tack, and Karl Knaths. The European artists included Picasso, Bonnard, Van Gogh, Henri Rousseau, Edouard Vuillard, Raoul Dufy, and Paul Klee.

36. Passantino and Martin, pp. 37–38; Parrott, "Phillips: Life and Writings," n.p.

37. Parrott and Research Office staff, "Chronology of Acquisitions," n.p.

38. Harth, pp. 43–44, 60–61.

39. During his stay in Detroit, Rivera was commissioned by Tannahill to paint his portrait, which was included in an exhibition of Rivera's work at the modern art gallery of the Detroit Society of Arts and Crafts. Jacob, pp. 164–65.

40. Harth, pp. 45–46, 61–62.

41. *Ibid.*, p. 67; Jacob, p. 166.

42. Tannahill, quoted in Harth, p. 61; on paintings, see p. 62.

43. *Ibid.*, pp. 46–47; Joy Hakanson Colby, "The Detroit Society of Arts and Crafts 1906–1976: An Introduction," in *Arts and Crafts in Detroit 1906–1976*, p. 155.

44. Harth, p. 47.

45. *Ibid.*, p. 45.

46. *Ibid.*, pp. 66–67; Sterne, pp. 297–98.

47. Colby, p. 31.

48. Jacob, pp. 158–59.

49. Tannahill's first show at the modern art gallery of the Detroit Society of Arts and Crafts, *American Folk Art, Painting, and Sculpture*, was drawn from Edith Halpert's Folk Art Gallery in New York, which opened in 1931.

50. Harth, p. 49; Jacob, p. 162.

51. Tannahill to Pierre Matisse, December 28, 1934, quoted in Jacob, pp. 166–67.

52. Harth, p. 115; Jacob, p. 167.

53. Harth, pp. 56–58; Jacob, pp. 167–68.

54. Jacob, p. 166.

55. *Ibid.*, p. 171.

56. Parrott, "Phillips: Life and Writings," n.p.; "Exhibitions at The Phillips Collection."

57. "Exhibitions at The Phillips Collection."

58. Maura K. Parrott and Research Office staff, "Chronology of Acquisitions," n.p.

59. "Exhibitions at The Phillips Collection."

60. Passantino, p. 562.

61. Phillips, quoted by Marjorie Phillips, *Duncan Phillips and His Collection*, Boston (Little, Brown) 1970, p. 304.

62. Harth, pp. 21, 23, 77–79.

63. Sterne, pp. 299–303.

64. Harth, pp. 79–81.

65. Sterne, p. 328.

66. Harth, pp. 82–84, 89.

67. *Ibid.*, pp. 90–91.

68. Sterne, p. 328.

69. Harth, p. 92.

70. *Ibid.*, pp. 92–94.

71. Purchase dates are not known for most of Tannahill's sculptures, but we do know that he purchased Constantin Brancusi's *Sleeping Child* in the 1930s, which demonstrates an advanced taste for this artist. Harth, pp. 110–46.

72. *Ibid.*, pp. 95–96. Tannahill's specification for acquiring work before 1925 reflected his preference for representational art.

73. *Ibid.*, pp. 109–10, 113, 124–25.

74. Phillips, "The Enchantment of Art," in Passantino, p. 204.

75. Harth, p. 110.

76. Both collectors acquired a more aggressive later work: Tannahill, a more distorted portrait of Dora Maar from 1939; Phillips, a bullfight scene from 1934.

77. After purchasing a watercolor by Emil Nolde in 1920, his first acquisition of modern art, Tannahill went on to buy works by Max Beckmann, Otto Dix, Lyonel Feininger, George Grosz, Käthe Kollwitz, Wilhem Lehmbruck, Paula Modersohn-Becker, Otto Mueller, Franz Marc, and Karl Schmidt-Rottluff; see Harth, pp. 25–26. Many of these artists were not collected by Phillips. In 1937, Phillips bought two watercolors by Grosz, but it was not until the 1940s that he added Kandinsky, Feininger, and Kollwitz to his collection.

78. Phillips first purchased Klee's work in that year and eventually acquired thirteen works for the collection; see Passantino, p. 282. Tannahill bought seven watercolors by Klee, the first from the 1940 exhibition at the Detroit Society of Arts and Crafts, the rest during the decade; see Harth, pp. 140–41.

79. Passantino, p. 268.

80. Harth, pp. 80–81.

81. Phillips acquired two non-objective paintings by Mondrian. Of *Composition No. 3* (1921 or 1922, repainted in 1925), he wrote, "I do not think I could find a better Mondrian, one more tonic and satisfying to one's inner need for balance and perfect relations." Phillips to Valentine Dudensing, May 1946, in Passantino, p. 278.

82. Harth, pp. 71–72, 106.

83. *Ibid.*, p. 108.

Additional References Consulted

Brewer, John, *The Consumption of Culture 1600–1800: Image, Object, Text*, London and New York (Routledge) 1995

Elsner, James, and Roger Cardinal (eds.), *The Culture of Collecting*, Cambridge, MA (Harvard University Press) 1994

Detroit Institute of Arts, The, *The Robert Hudson Tannahill Bequest to The Detroit Institute of Arts*, Detroit (The Detroit Institute of Arts) 1970

Muensterberger, Werner, *Collecting – An Unruly Passion: Psychological Perspectives*, Princeton, NJ (Princeton University Press) 1994

Pearce, Susan, *On Collecting: An Investigation into Collecting in the European Tradition*, London and New York (Routledge) 1995

Rewald, John, *Cézanne and America: Dealers, Collectors, Artists and Critics, 1891–1921*, Washington, D.C. (The National Gallery of Art: The A.W. Mellon Lectures in the Fine Arts) 1979

Saarinen, Aline B., *The Proud Possessors*, New York (Random House) 1958

Constantin Brancusi

(1876–1957)

Sleeping Child, c. 1906–08

bronze

14.6 × 10.8 × 14 cm

(5¾ × 4¼ × 5½ in.)

THE DETROIT INSTITUTE OF ARTS

BEQUEST OF ROBERT H. TANNAHILL

Jean-Baptiste Carpeaux

(1827–1875)

Head of a Child, 1850–60

bronze

19.4 × 14.6 × 15.9 cm

(7⅝ × 5¾ × 6¼ in.)

THE DETROIT INSTITUTE OF ARTS

BEQUEST OF ROBERT H. TANNAHILL

Wilhelm Lehmbruck

(1881–1919)

Seated Girl, 1913–14

bronze

27.9 × 44.8 × 14 cm

(11 × 17⅝ × 5½ in.)

The Detroit Institute of Arts

Bequest of Robert H. Tannahill

Henri Matisse
(1869–1954)
Seated Nude, 1909
bronze
29.2 × 15.6 × 21.6 cm
(11½ × 6⅛ × 8½ in.)
THE DETROIT INSTITUTE OF ARTS
BEQUEST OF ROBERT H. TANNAHILL

Auguste Rodin

(1840–1917)

Baudelaire, 1898

bronze

22.5 × 20 × 22.9 cm

(8⅞ × 7⅞ × 9 in.)

THE DETROIT INSTITUTE OF ARTS

BEQUEST OF ROBERT H. TANNAHILL

Auguste Rodin

(1840–1917)

Brother and Sister, 1890

bronze

38.1 × 17.7 × 15.8 cm

(15 × 7 × 6¼ in.)

WASHINGTON, D.C.

THE PHILLIPS COLLECTION

GIFT FROM THE ESTATE OF

KATHERINE S. DREIER, 1953

LEFT

Max Beckmann

(1884–1950)

Self-Portrait in Olive and Brown, 1945

oil on canvas

60.3 × 49.9 cm

(23¾ × 19⅝ in.)

THE DETROIT INSTITUTE OF ARTS

GIFT OF ROBERT H. TANNAHILL

RIGHT

Paul Cézanne

(1839–1906)

Self-Portrait, 1878–80

oil on canvas

60.4 × 47 cm

(23¾ × 18½ in.)

WASHINGTON, D.C.

THE PHILLIPS COLLECTION

Paul Gauguin

(1848–1903)

Self-Portrait, c. 1893

oil on canvas

46.2 × 38.1 cm

(18³⁄₁₆ × 15 in.)

The Detroit Institute of Arts

Gift of Robert H. Tannahill

Piet Mondrian

(1870–1944)

Self-Portrait, c. 1900

oil on canvas, mounted on

hardboard

50.7 × 39.3 cm

(20 × 15½ in.)

Washington, D.C.

The Phillips Collection

Hilaire-Germain-Edgar Degas
(1834–1917)
Melancholy, late 1860s
oil on canvas
19 × 24.7 cm
(7½ × 9¾ in.)
Washington, D.C.
The Phillips Collection

LEFT

Hilaire-Germain-Edgar Degas

(1834–1917)

Woman with a Headband,
1870–72

oil on canvas

33 × 24.8 cm

(13 × 9¾ in.)

THE DETROIT INSTITUTE OF ARTS

BEQUEST OF ROBERT H. TANNAHILL

RIGHT

Paula Modersohn-Becker

(1876–1907)

Old Peasant Woman, c. 1905

oil on canvas

75.6 × 57.8 cm

(29¾ × 22¾ in.)

THE DETROIT INSTITUTE OF ARTS

GIFT OF ROBERT H. TANNAHILL

Hilaire-Germain-Edgar Degas

(1834–1917)

Women Combing Their Hair,

c. 1875–76

oil on paper mounted on

canvas

32.4 × 46.2 cm

(12¾ × 18⅛ in.)

WASHINGTON, D.C.

THE PHILLIPS COLLECTION

Pierre-Auguste Renoir

(1841–1919)

Seated Bather, 1903–06

oil on canvas

116.2 × 88.9 cm

(45¾ × 35 in.)

THE DETROIT INSTITUTE OF ARTS

BEQUEST OF ROBERT H. TANNAHILL

Hilaire-Germain-Edgar Degas

(1834–1917)

Violinist and Young Woman, c. 1871

oil on canvas

46.4 × 55.9 cm

(18¼ × 22 in.)

THE DETROIT INSTITUTE OF ARTS

BEQUEST OF ROBERT H. TANNAHILL

Hilaire-Germain-Edgar Degas

(1834–1917)

Dancers at the Bar, c. 1900

oil on canvas

130.1 × 97.7 cm

(51¼ × 38½ in.)

WASHINGTON, D.C.

THE PHILLIPS COLLECTION

Jean-Auguste-Dominique
Ingres
(1780–1867)
Perseus and Andromeda,
c. 1819
oil on canvas
19.7 × 16.2 cm
(7¾ × 6⅜ in.)
THE DETROIT INSTITUTE OF ARTS
BEQUEST OF ROBERT H. TANNAHILL

Jean-Auguste-Dominique Ingres
(1780–1867)
Portrait of Marie Marcoz
(later Vicomtesse de Senonnes),
1813
pencil on wove paper
27 × 20.1 cm
(10⅝ × 7⅞ in.)
THE DETROIT INSTITUTE OF ARTS
BEQUEST OF ROBERT H. TANNAHILL

Jean-Auguste-Dominique
Ingres
(1780–1867)
The Small Bather, 1826
oil on canvas
32.7 × 25 cm
(12⅞ × 9⅞ in.)
WASHINGTON, D.C.
THE PHILLIPS COLLECTION

Paul Cézanne

(1839–1906)

Bathers, c. 1880

oil on canvas

34.6 × 38.1 cm

(13⅝ × 15 in.)

THE DETROIT INSTITUTE OF ARTS

BEQUEST OF ROBERT H. TANNAHILL

Edouard Manet

(1832–1883)

On the Beach, 1873

oil on canvas

40 × 48.9 cm

(15¾ × 19¼ in.)

THE DETROIT INSTITUTE OF ARTS

BEQUEST OF ROBERT H. TANNAHILL

Vincent van Gogh

(1853–1890)

Bank of the Oise at Auvers, 1890

oil on canvas

73.3 × 93.7 cm

(28⅞ × 36⅞ in.)

THE DETROIT INSTITUTE OF ARTS

BEQUEST OF ROBERT H. TANNAHILL

Vincent van Gogh

(1853–1890)

The Diggers, 1889

oil on canvas

65.1 × 50.2 cm

(25⅛ × 19¼ in.)

THE DETROIT INSTITUTE OF ARTS

BEQUEST OF ROBERT H. TANNAHILL

Vincent van Gogh

(1853–1890)

The Road Menders, 1889

oil on canvas

73.7 × 92.8

(29 × 36½ in.)

Washington, D.C.

The Phillips Collection

Vincent van Gogh

(1853–1890)

Entrance to the Public

Gardens in Arles, 1888

oil on canvas

72.3 × 90.8 cm

(28½ × 35¾ in.)

WASHINGTON, D.C.

THE PHILLIPS COLLECTION

Honoré Daumier

(1808–1879)

Children Playing, n.d.,

dark-brown ink and

watercolor on paper

15.2 × 21.3

(6¼ × 8⅜ in.)

The Detroit Institute of Arts

Bequest of Robert H. Tannahill

Honoré Daumier
(1808–1879)
Figure of a Woman and
Woman with Child, n.d.
dark-brown ink and
watercolor on paper
15.2 × 21.3
(6¼ × 8⅛ in.)
THE DETROIT INSTITUTE OF ARTS
BEQUEST OF ROBERT H. TANNAHILL

Honoré Daumier

(1808–1879)

The Family, 1860s

watercolor, black chalk,

graphite, and white

highlights on paper

17.1 × 19 cm

(6¾ × 7½ in.)

WASHINGTON, D.C.

THE PHILLIPS COLLECTION

Honoré Daumier

(1808–1879)

To the Street, 1840–50

oil on wood panel

27.3 × 21.5 cm

(10¾ × 8½ in.)

WASHINGTON, D.C.

THE PHILLIPS COLLECTION

Henri de Toulouse-Lautrec

(1864–1901)

At the Circus, 1899

black chalk, crayon, and gray

wash on wove paper

25.2 × 35.6 cm

(9¹⁵⁄₁₆ × 14 in.)

THE DETROIT INSTITUTE OF ARTS

BEQUEST OF ROBERT H. TANNAHILL

LEFT

Henri de Toulouse-Lautrec

(1864–1901)

La Loge: A Performance of

"Faust," 1896

lithograph

38.1 × 27.9 cm

(15 × 11 in.)

WASHINGTON, D.C.

THE PHILLIPS COLLECTION

RIGHT

Henri de Toulouse-Lautrec

(1864–1901)

Miss May Belfort, state 1,

1895

color lithograph

54.6 × 42.2 cm

(21½ × 16⅝ in.) image

WASHINGTON, D.C.

THE PHILLIPS COLLECTION

Paul Klee

(1879–1940)

Arrival of the Jugglers, 1926

oil on incised putty on

cardboard mounted on

cardboard

17.4 × 27.3 cm

(6⅞ × 10¾ in.)

WASHINGTON, D.C.

THE PHILLIPS COLLECTION

Paul Klee

(1879–1940)

Captive Pierrot, 1923

watercolor on heavy paper

mounted on gray cardboard

39.7 × 30.2 cm

(15⅛ × 11⅞ in.)

THE DETROIT INSTITUTE OF ARTS

BEQUEST OF ROBERT H. TANNAHILL

Henri Matisse

(1869–1954)

Seated Female Nude, n.d.

black crayon on paper

62.9 × 47.6 cm

(24¹³⁄₁₆ × 18¾ in.)

THE DETROIT INSTITUTE OF ARTS

BEQUEST OF ROBERT H. TANNAHILL

Henri Matisse

(1869–1954)

Untitled (Seated Nude), 1908

ink on paper

27 × 20.9 cm

(10⅝ × 8¼ in.)

WASHINGTON, D.C.

THE PHILLIPS COLLECTION

GIFT OF MARJORIE PHILLIPS, 1984

Henri Matisse

(1869–1954)

Coffee, 1916

oil on canvas

100.7 × 65.4 cm

(39⅝ × 25¾ in.)

THE DETROIT INSTITUTE OF ARTS

BEQUEST OF ROBERT H. TANNAHILL

LEFT

Amedeo Modigliani

(1884–1920)

Young Man with a Cap,

20th century

oil on canvas

61 × 37.8 cm

(24 × 14⅞ in.)

THE DETROIT INSTITUTE OF ARTS

BEQUEST OF ROBERT H. TANNAHILL

RIGHT

Amedeo Modigliani

(1884–1920)

A Man, 20th century

oil on canvas

46 × 38.1 cm

(18⅛ × 15 in.)

THE DETROIT INSTITUTE OF ARTS

BEQUEST OF ROBERT H. TANNAHILL

Amedeo Modigliani
(1884–1920)
Elena Povolozky, 1917
oil on canvas
64.6 × 48.5 cm
(25½ × 19⅛ in.)
WASHINGTON, D.C.
THE PHILLIPS COLLECTION

Otto Mueller

(1874–1930)

Two Bathers, 1928–30

crayon, pastel, watercolor,

and brush and black ink on

off-white wove paper

52 × 68.5 cm

(20½ × 27 in.)

THE DETROIT INSTITUTE OF ARTS

BEQUEST OF ROBERT H. TANNAHILL

Otto Dix

(1891–1969)

Portrait of the Artist's Son

Ursus, 1931

watercolor and graphite

pencil on cream wove paper

56.4 × 39 cm

(22¼ × 15⅜ in.)

THE DETROIT INSTITUTE OF ARTS

BEQUEST OF ROBERT H. TANNAHILL

Pablo Picasso

(1881–1973)

Woman's Head, 1945

lithograph, 50/50

30.8 × 23.4 cm

(12⅛ × 9¼ in.)

Washington, D.C.

The Phillips Collection

Pablo Picasso

(1881–1973)

Seated Woman, 1924

lithograph, 11/50

38.1 × 27.9 cm

(15 × 11 in.) sheet

29.8 × 21.5 cm

(11¾ × 8½ in.) image

Washington, D.C.

The Phillips Collection

Gift of Marjorie Phillips, 1984

Pablo Picasso

(1881–1973)

Three Bathers, Juan-les-Pins,
1920

graphite pencil on wove paper

27.3 × 42.1 cm

(10⅜ × 13¾ in.)

THE DETROIT INSTITUTE OF ARTS

BEQUEST OF ROBERT H. TANNAHILL

Pablo Picasso

(1881–1973)

Woman Seated in an
Armchair, 1923

oil on canvas

130.2 × 97.2 cm

(51¼ × 38¼ in.)

THE DETROIT INSTITUTE OF ARTS

BEQUEST OF ROBERT H. TANNAHILL

Pablo Picasso

(1881–1973)

Melancholy Woman, 1902

oil on canvas

100 × 69.2 cm

(39⅜ × 27¼ in.)

THE DETROIT INSTITUTE OF ARTS

BEQUEST OF ROBERT H. TANNAHILL

Pablo Picasso

(1881–1973)

The Blue Room, 1901

oil on canvas

50.4 × 61.5 cm

(19⅞ × 24¼ in.)

Washington, D.C.

The Phillips Collection

Pablo Picasso

(1881–1973)

Head of a Harlequin, 1905

oil on canvas

40.6 × 33 cm

(16 × 13 in.)

The Detroit Institute of Arts

Bequest of Robert H. Tannahill

Georges Rouault

(1871–1958)

The Clown, c. 1907

gouache and oil on board

57.2 × 50.8 cm

(22½ × 20 in.)

THE DETROIT INSTITUTE OF ARTS

BEQUEST OF ROBERT H. TANNAHILL

Georges Rouault

(1871–1958)

Standing Nude, 1909

watercolor and oil on

cardboard

99.1 × 63.2 cm

(35⅞ × 24⅞ in.)

THE DETROIT INSTITUTE OF ARTS

BEQUEST OF ROBERT H. TANNAHILL

Chaim Soutine

(1893–1943)

Little Girl, 20th century

oil on canvas

54.9 × 43.2 cm

(21⅜ × 17 in.)

THE DETROIT INSTITUTE OF ARTS

BEQUEST OF ROBERT H. TANNAHILL

Chaim Soutine

(1893–1943)

Woman in Profile, 1937

oil on canvas

46.6 × 27.6 cm

(18⅜ × 10⅞ in.)

WASHINGTON, D.C.

THE PHILLIPS COLLECTION

Henry Moore
(1898–1986)
Figures in a Setting, 1942
wax crayon, watercolor, pen
and ink, white gouache, and
graphite on wove paper
36.5 × 51.6 cm
(14⅜ × 20¼ in.)
Washington, D.C.
The Phillips Collection

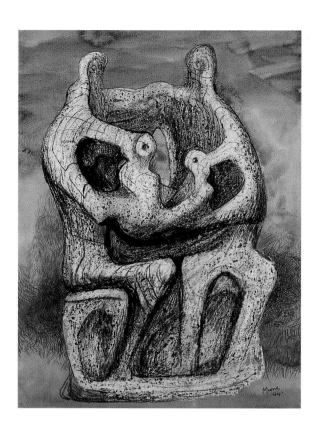

Henry Moore

(1898–1986)

Family Group No. 2, 1944

watercolor over pencil

and ink

46.4 × 36.2 cm

(18¼ × 14⅛ in.)

THE DETROIT INSTITUTE OF ARTS

BEQUEST OF ROBERT H. TANNAHILL

Henry Moore

(1898–1986)

Family Group, 1946

bronze

44.3 × 33.2 × 22 cm

(17½ × 13 × 8⅜ in.)

WASHINGTON, D.C.

THE PHILLIPS COLLECTION

Some Personal Reminiscences

Robert Hudson Tannahill:

Charles H. Sawyer

I first met Robert Tannahill in 1932 at a meeting of the American Association of Museums in Detroit. I was then the young and inexperienced curator of the Addison Gallery of American Art at Phillips Academy, Andover, Massachusetts, attending my first museum meeting. I stayed in Grosse Pointe with a family who were friends and neighbors of Tannahill and also of the Edsel Fords. My meeting with Tannahill was casual; he was then a trustee, patron, and honorary curator of American art at The Detroit Institute of Arts. I learned from members of the staff of his active involvement in the Detroit Society of Arts and Crafts, which in its educational and exhibition activities had become the major sponsor of contemporary art in Detroit and supporter of local artists.

My principal recollection of that visit was joining a small group on a trip to Dearborn to view Greenfield Village and the collections assembled under the guidance of Henry Ford Sr. and his son Edsel. It was still a private collection at the time and in a formative stage, but most impressive in its size and variety of buildings and collections. When it entered the public domain soon afterward, Tannahill, a cousin of Mrs. Edsel Ford and close friend of the family, became a trustee. Twenty years later, the library of the Henry Ford Museum was named the Robert Hudson Tannahill Research Library

Diego Rivera
Portrait of Robert H. Tannahill, 1932
(DETAIL; SEE PAGE 123)

Interior views of Robert Hudson Tannahill's residence,
October 1969.

in his honor, reflecting his lifelong interest in American art and the decorative arts.

In 1936 I returned to Detroit, staying in Grosse Pointe with the same family whose house formed part of an enclave adjacent to the Russell Alger House, later the Grosse Pointe War Memorial, which had become a branch of The Detroit Institute of Arts. Perry Rathbone, who had earlier served for two years as assistant to Dr. William Valentiner, the director of The Detroit Institute of Arts, was the curator in charge. I had known Perry previously when we both were enrolled in Professor Paul Sach's museum course at Harvard; Perry subsequently became director of the St. Louis Art Museum and later director of the Museum of Fine Arts in Boston. During that visit, at a reception at Alger House, Dr. Valentiner's residence at the time, I met Tannahill and learned that we had two experiences in common.

First, Tannahill had been a primary sponsor in bringing selections from the Lillie P. Bliss collection, on loan from the Museum of Modern Art (MoMA), New York, to Detroit in 1933 under the auspices of the Society of Arts and Crafts. Her collection contained significant examples of works by artists who were to form the nucleus of his own collection of modern art, including Pablo Picasso, Paul Cézanne, Henri Matisse, and others in the French

tradition. Miss Bliss, a close friend of Andover's major benefactor, had been a member of the Art Committee of the Addison Gallery and was influential in the formation of its collection. After her death, we showed her collection at the Addison Gallery in the fall of 1931, following its exhibition in New York.

Second, Tannahill was a prime sponsor of the Detroit Committee of the Museum of Modern Art, New York. I, in turn, had been a member of the Boston Committee in 1933. (Later, the resulting Boston affiliate of MoMA became, after considerable semantic discussion of the term "modern," the Institute of Contemporary Art.) Both committees were involved primarily in the circulation of exhibitions and collections from MoMA, with which at that time we both had a close association.

I did not see the Tannahill collection during either of those visits but became aware of it through friends in the Detroit area and staff members of The Detroit Institute of Arts. Also, when visiting New York art dealers, I learned of the breadth of his collecting interests. Edith Halpert of the Downtown Gallery, who had collaborated in several of the exhibitions he had arranged for the Detroit Society of Arts and Crafts, praised his discriminating taste. He acquired a number of works from these exhibitions, including watercolors

by John Marin and Charles Demuth, as well as examples of folk art from a comprehensive exhibition at the Society of Arts and Crafts in 1932.

The Depression years of the 1930s were a very difficult time for the city of Detroit and its cultural institutions, including The Detroit Institute of Arts. After the failure of the banks in 1933, the city withdrew almost all its financial support, many staff members were placed on unpaid furlough, and open hours were substantially curtailed. It became the responsibility of a few sponsors with substantial means, including Tannahill, to fill this gap and restore gradually something close to normal activity by the end of the decade. From all accounts, his own resources were not materially diminished during this period, enabling his collecting activities to continue unabated.

I had no personal contact with Tannahill during the 1940s but learned subsequently from friends and relatives in the Detroit area that it was a very difficult period for him. The death of Edsel Ford in 1943 was a grievous blow from which he never completely recovered. He became increasingly withdrawn and remote, although continuing his active interest and involvement in The Detroit Institute of Arts and the Society of Arts and Crafts. His collection continued to grow during this period, although at a slower pace. At the same time, his association with his cousin Eleanor Clay Ford became closer. They shared common interests such as traveling to New York together accompanied by members of the curatorial staff of The Detroit Institute of Arts to visit art dealers.

My own association with Detroit was more remote during this period. I left Andover in 1940 to become director of the Worcester Art Museum in Worcester, Massachusetts. Three years later, I entered government service, spending a year in England in the Military Government for Germany and, later, Office of Strategic Services (OSS). During the final year of the Second World War, I was in Washington as assistant secretary for the Commission for the Preservation of Monuments and Works of Art in War Areas. In 1947–48 I became director of the Division of the Arts at Yale and visited Detroit several times on fundraising efforts in ensuing years. On one of these visits, in 1950, I stayed in Grosse Pointe with a family who were close friends of Tannahill. This afforded me my first opportunity to see his recently completed house and collection.

We spent an evening there with a few other friends. Number 22 Lee Gate Lane is, in its architecture, a modest departure from the prevailing Tudor and Georgian

Interior views of Robert Hudson Tannahill's residence,
October 1969.

mansions of the 1930s and 1940s in the Grosse Pointe area. Sparse in its decoration and somewhat Cubist in form, the house seemed to reflect contemporary design as practiced by architects trained at the Bauhaus. The interior reflected much more specifically Tannahill's particular vision and taste. As Marjorie Harth observes in her dissertation on Tannahill, he was involved in all aspects of planning the house, especially its interior design. She quotes Polly Jessup, his consultant for interior decoration, that Tannahill was involved in all the details including paint color, fabrics, and the placement of furniture and decorative objects. In contrast to most of her clients, for whom works of art were part of the decoration, in Tannahill's house they became a primary focus.

On entering the house you faced, in the foyer, a wall with a large figure drawing, *Pomona* by Georges Braque, as the centerpiece, with a self-portrait by Paul Gauguin (see illus., p. 76) and *Head of a Harlequin* by Picasso (see illus., p. 109) on either side. On the staircase to the right was Picasso's monumental *Woman Seated in an Armchair* (see illus., p. 106). Fred Cummings quotes Tannahill as referring to it as "the mistress of the house." Next to it, the *Melancholy Woman* of Picasso's Blue Period (see illus., p. 107) added to a general, almost overpowering feeling of monumentality and an emphasis on line and

form that characterized the collection as a whole. The foyer also contained a few pieces of small sculpture and decorative objects, all in excellent taste but definitely subordinate to the paintings. The living-room was dominated by the sober *Portrait of Madame Cézanne* on one wall, the artist's smaller *Mont Sainte-Victoire* (see illus., p. 30) at one end, and two Degas portraits at the other. Across from the Cézanne portrait, Renoir's *Seated Bather* (see illus., p. 81) provided a somewhat lighter touch to the room.

The dining-room had a lighter and more colorful ambiance, with the vibrant *Poppies* by Matisse (see illus., p. 131) providing the focus of one wall and a Georges Seurat landscape (see illus., p. 27) another. Both library and study were more somber in tone; I recall especially the small and challenging *Three Skulls* by Cézanne and Georges Rouault's *Portrait of Josephine Baker* and *The Clown* (see illus., p. 110) in the study. These three works reflect the many and sometimes contrasting aspects of Tannahill's taste. I felt his treatment of the public areas had been carefully planned and may have been influenced – in design if not in subject-matter – by his enthusiasm for and involvement in the theatrical arts.

The works of art on the second floor were in a sense more private, and revealed Tannahill's personal taste, the

breadth of his vision, and his ability to discern quality in a variety of media and forms of expression. Beside his bed was the superb portrait drawing by Jean-Auguste-Dominique Ingres of Marie Marcoz (see illus., p. 85), and across the room was a haunting Cubist-period still life by Picasso. In another bedroom I observed the delightful *Four-Leaf Clover* of 1873 by Winslow Homer, and contemporary watercolors and drawings.

In the storage area were many objects in a variety of media that Tannahill took particular pleasure in showing to his friends and on occasion to students and members of the curatorial staff of The Detroit Institute of Arts. These included small bronzes, which he also installed in various niches throughout the house, and African sculpture and objects in various media that he continued to collect over a period of thirty years. Like the bronzes, they were of modest size but superb in quality, with a rich patina that distinguished them from many collections of African art formed at about the same time. Most impressive of all to me were the drawings and watercolors, both European and American, by artists as diverse as John Marin, Emil Nolde, and Paul Klee. The Klees were especially noteworthy, for they revealed a discernment of a very subjective and abstract form of art dismissed by many collectors of the time as "doodles."

I became better acquainted with the Tannahill collection during visits with members of my museum practice classes at the University of Michigan during the 1960s. Sam Sachs, now director of the Frick Collection, who became director of The Detroit Institute of Arts in the mid-1980s, reminds me that he accompanied one of these classes in 1963 when he was assistant director of the University of Michigan Museum of Art. These visits continued annually through 1968. A gracious host, Tannahill laid out firm ground rules, for example that we could bring only twenty people at a time, including faculty members who sometimes accompanied us. In retrospect, I think these visits represented a major concession on his part because he was a very private man at this stage of his life and wanted no publication or recognition of his collection. For example, he insisted on anonymity when lending objects for exhibition at The Detroit Institute of Arts.

Another pleasant association I had with Tannahill during those years came about accidentally. I had the habit of visiting The Detroit Institute of Arts occasionally on Sunday mornings when the galleries were practically empty, both to prepare for class visits and to become better acquainted with the collections. I discovered Tannahill had a similar habit; on several occasions we toured the galleries together. I was

Interior views of Robert Hudson Tannahill's residence,
October 1969.

tremendously impressed with the scope and depth of his
knowledge and his pride in the collections. He had the
eye of both a connoisseur and a curator, as well as an
ability to be critical at times of the installation of
individual exhibitions. Tannahill seemed to enjoy
especially the decorative arts galleries, having begun his
initial collecting in this field in the 1920s, and the
graphic arts gallery, in which he took great pride and
from which he derived much satisfaction. Although a
new generation of trustees and staff had taken over
primary responsibility for the museum's administration
and policies in the 1960s, it was clear to me that The
Detroit Institute of Arts and its collections remained
central to his life and interests.

My other impressions of Tannahill came largely through
the experience of Paul Grigaut, who in 1946 had become
a curator and then chief curator in the administration of
Edgar Richardson, who succeeded Dr. Valentiner in 1946
when the latter became director of the Los Angeles
County Museum of Art. I had known Grigaut when he
was a professor of French at the University of New
Hampshire in the 1930s. Grigaut, with a profound
interest in the visual arts and collecting, enrolled in Paul
Sachs's museum course at Harvard University, and
subsequently, during the Second World War, served in
the State Department as a liaison to the Arts and

Monuments Preservation Commission, of which I was
the assistant secretary.

Grigaut soon became a friend and confidant of Tannahill
and frequently accompanied him and Eleanor Ford on
their visits to New York art galleries. Like Tannahill, he
was a man of broad taste and vision with a particular
affinity for French culture and expertise in the decorative
arts. They were, in many respects, kindred spirits: both
very private people, different in personality and social
background, but with mutual respect. With the arrival of
a new administration, Grigaut left Detroit in 1963, and
two years later joined me as associate director of the
University of Michigan Museum of Art. During that
period, he continued to maintain a close association with
Tannahill and to accompany him on his visits to New
York. While very protective of his relationship, Grigaut
shared with me his profound respect for Tannahill's taste
and judgment of works of art.

In January 1969, Grigaut died suddenly after a severe
stroke. That spring, Tannahill came to Ann Arbor in the
company of Fred Cummings, then curator of European
Art, and Alvan McCauley Jr., an influential trustee of
The Detroit Institute of Arts and close friend of
Tannahill in Grosse Pointe, to see the memorial
exhibition we had arranged in Grigaut's honor and to

Diego Rivera

(1886–1957)

Portrait of Robert H. Tannahill, 1932

oil on canvas

88.3 × 69.9 cm

(34¾ × 27½ in.)

The Detroit Institute of Arts

Bequest of Robert H. Tannahill

make selections of objects to be acquired for The Detroit Institute of Arts's collections. The Grigaut collection, like Tannahill's, revealed a wide range of periods and interests, and it demonstrated what a collector of exquisite taste, but modest means, could assemble. This was my last meeting with Tannahill; he died the following September. I cherish these memories of a distinguished gentleman, collector, and art connoisseur.

Because I knew them both, although at different times and in different frames of reference, I have been asked to make some comparisons between Robert Tannahill and Duncan Phillips and comment on the evolution of their collections. I find many parallels and some differences between the two. As becomes clear in the monumental study *The Eye of Duncan Phillips: A Collection in the Making*,[1] Phillips's taste evolved throughout his career, becoming both more adventurous and more discriminating. Although Tannahill had contacts with artists in the Detroit area, his collection was more influenced by his association with Dr. Valentiner, and later with Grigaut, and by his visits to New York art galleries. In a primary sense, however, both

Phillips and Tannahill were independent, essentially private individuals, who made their own judgment of works of art.

It is interesting to observe how many parallels exist in the works represented in their collections. In both cases their taste seems to have been predominantly in the French tradition, highlighted in The Phillips Collection in the monumental *Luncheon of the Boating Party* by Renoir (see illus., p. 21) and the wonderful works by Bonnard, and in the Tannahill collection by Picasso's *Woman Seated in an Armchair* and *Melancholy Woman* (see illus., pp. 106 and 107). They were united in acquiring major works by Paul Klee and, among American artists, John Marin and Charles Demuth.

By way of contrast, as I have observed earlier, works in the Tannahill collection seemed to emphasize predominantly line and form where, in contrast, The Phillips Collection reflects a more painterly vision and emphasis on color. Especially with the addition of the gallery devoted to Mark Rothko, The Phillips Collection is the more adventurous. Overall, however, I think that Phillips and Tannahill were kindred spirits with keen perception, exquisite taste, and a dedication to bringing their private collections into the public domain.

In preparing these informal and highly subjective observations, I owe a particular obligation to my former student, colleague, and friend, Marjorie Harth, for providing me with access to her dissertation on Tannahill and especially for refreshing my memory of his collection as it was installed in his house. I am also grateful to Mary Jane Jacob, another former student at the University of Michigan, for her discerning comments on Tannahill's association with the Society of Arts and Crafts. I also wish to acknowledge the assistance of Ellen Sharp, curator of graphic arts at The Detroit Institute of Arts, and of Samuel Sachs for reviewing the manuscript.

1 Erika D. Passantino and David W. Scott (eds.), *The Eye of Duncan Phillips: A Collection in the Making*, New Haven, CT (The Phillips Collection in association with Yale University Press) 1999

Franz Marc

(1880–1916)

Animals in a Landscape, 1914

oil on canvas

110.2 × 99.7 cm

(43⅜ × 39¼ in.)

THE DETROIT INSTITUTE OF ARTS

GIFT OF ROBERT H. TANNAHILL

Franz Marc

(1880–1916)

Deer in the Forest I, 1913

oil on canvas

100.9 × 104.7 cm

(39¾ × 41¼ in.)

WASHINGTON, D.C.

THE PHILLIPS COLLECTION

Emil Nolde

(1867–1956)

Tulips and Bird, c. 1920

watercolor on Japanese paper

34.9 × 48.6 cm

(13¾ × 19⅛ in.)

THE DETROIT INSTITUTE OF ARTS

BEQUEST OF ROBERT H. TANNAHILL

Morris Graves

(born 1910)

Young Gander Ready for Flight, 1952

oil on canvas

121.9 × 84.4 cm

(48 × 33¼ in.)

Washington, D.C.

The Phillips Collection

Pablo Picasso

(1881–1973)

Bottle of Anis del Mono, 1915

oil on canvas

46 × 54.6 cm

(18⅛ × 21½ in.)

THE DETROIT INSTITUTE OF ARTS

BEQUEST OF ROBERT H. TANNAHILL

Pablo Picasso

(1881–1973)

Abstraction, Biarritz, 1918

oil on canvas

35.5 × 27.3 cm

(14¼ × 10¾ in.)

WASHINGTON, D.C.

THE PHILLIPS COLLECTION

Henri Matisse

(1869–1954)

Poppies, c. 1919

oil on canvas

100.7 × 81.3 cm

(39⅝ × 32 in.)

THE DETROIT INSTITUTE OF ARTS

BEQUEST OF ROBERT H. TANNAHILL

Henri Matisse

(1869–1954)

*Interior with Egyptian
Curtain,* 1948

oil on canvas

116.3 × 89.2 cm

(45¾ × 35⅛ in.)

WASHINGTON, D.C.

THE PHILLIPS COLLECTION

Diego Rivera

(1886–1957)

Still Life with Carafe,

Knife, and Chestnuts,

1918

pencil on paper

31.4 × 23.3 cm

(12⅜ × 9³⁄₁₆ in.)

THE DETROIT INSTITUTE

OF ARTS

BEQUEST OF ROBERT H.

TANNAHILL

Henri Matisse

(1869–1954)

Studio, Quai St. Michel,

1916

oil on canvas

147.9 × 116.8 cm

(58¼ × 46 in.)

WASHINGTON, D.C.

THE PHILLIPS COLLECTION

Robert Hudson Tannahill

A Chronology

1893
Robert Hudson Tannahill is born on 1 April to Elizabeth Ann Hudson and Robert Blythe Tannahill. His mother's family are the founders of the J.L. Hudson department store, where his father is vice-president.

1903
Tannahill travels to the East Coast on a buying trip with his mother, an early collector of American antique furniture.

1911–15
Tannahill attends the University of Michigan.

1913
Tannahill takes his first trip to Europe, mainly to France, which begins his lifelong interest in French language and culture. He travels with his cousins, Josephine and Eleanor Clay, daughters of his mother's sister, Eliza Hudson Clay. Josephine would go on to marry Ernest C. Kanzler, and Eleanor would marry Edsel Ford.

1916
Tannahill receives an M.A. from Harvard University.

1917–18
Tannahill does civilian army service as an interpreter at a base hospital in France.

1920
Tannahill makes his first purchase of modern art, a watercolor titled *The Steamer* by Emil Nolde.

1920–21
Tannahill writes four plays and secures copyright for two of them.

1921
Tannahill's mother dies, leaving him her entire estate.

c. 1921
Tannahill moves in with his mother's sister, Eliza Hudson Clay.

1924
William R. Valentiner is named the director of The Detroit Institute of Arts, having been a consultant since 1921.

1925
Tannahill's father dies and leaves him his entire estate. Hereafter, Tannahill receives a steady income from J.L. Hudson stock.

1927
The Detroit Institute of Arts names Tannahill honorary curator of American art.

1930
Because of his financial support to The Detroit Institute of Arts, Tannahill is named a benefactor of the Founders Society.

Tannahill invites Valentiner to accompany him to Europe.

1931
Tannahill is appointed a trustee of The Detroit Institute of Arts, a position he holds until his death.

Tannahill becomes the chairman of the Friends of Modern Art, organized at The Detroit Institute of Arts to encourage private collectors to buy modern art and to donate works to the museum.

Tannahill encourages the Detroit Society of Arts and Crafts to open a modern art gallery.

1932
The Detroit Society of Arts and Crafts opens its modern art gallery.

Tannahill commissions Diego Rivera to paint his portrait and helps organize an exhibition of the artist's paintings and drawings for the modern art gallery of the Detroit Society of Arts and Crafts.

Tannahill exhibits some of his modern paintings at The Detroit Institute of Arts, the only documented occasion when he allows his name to be associated with his collection.

1933
At the modern art gallery of the Detroit Society of Arts and Crafts, Tannahill organizes the exhibition *Paintings from the Ambroise Vollard Collection*, borrowed from Knoedler & Co., New York. From the exhibition he acquires *Mont Sainte-Victoire* by Paul Cézanne (see illus., p. 30).

Robert Hudson Tannahill and Diego Rivera, 1932.

1934

Working with Pierre Matisse in New York, Tannahill and Valentiner organize an exhibition of work by Henri Matisse and Georges Rouault.

From his exhibition of work by John Marin and Georgia O'Keeffe, organized with the assistance of Edith Halpert and Alfred Stieglitz, Tannahill purchases work by both artists.

1935

Tannahill organizes a folk art exhibition for The Detroit Institute of Arts, which relies on loans from New York collections.

Tannahill helps his cousin Josephine Kanzler start the Detroit Committee of the Museum of Modern Art, with the goal of promoting modern art outside New York City.

1936

Thirteen works from the Lillie P. Bliss collection are exhibited at the modern art gallery of the Detroit Society of Arts and Crafts. To demonstrate the influence of African sculpture on modern European art, Tannahill organizes a complementary exhibition of African art.

1940

Tannahill organizes an exhibition of watercolors and drawings by Pablo Picasso for the modern art gallery of the Detroit Society of Arts and Crafts.

Tannahill mounts an exhibition of Paul Klee's work for the society's modern art gallery.

Around this time, Tannahill suffers bouts of poor health.

1943

Tannahill is devastated by Edsel Ford's premature death. His cousin Eleanor Ford becomes dependent on Tannahill, who serves as her constant escort.

1944

Eliza Hudson Clay, Tannahill's housemate and aunt, dies. He lives alone for the rest of his life.

1945

Valentiner retires from The Detroit Institute of Arts and moves away from the city, depriving Tannahill of a close friend and confidant.

1946

Tannahill becomes the executive secretary of the Founders Society and the Arts Commission of The Detroit Institute of Arts.

1948

Tannahill moves into a new house in Grosse Pointe, built to showcase his collection.

1961

Tannahill establishes the Robert Tannahill Fund to help support his favorite non-profit organizations in Detroit.

1962

In poor health, Tannahill resigns from the Arts Commission.

1966

The American galleries at The Detroit Institute of Arts officially become the Robert Hudson Tannahill Wing of American Art.

1969

Tannahill dies of congestive heart failure on September 25.

1970

The Detroit Institute of Arts opens the exhibition *A Collector's Treasure: The Tannahill Bequest*, accompanied by a catalogue of his complete bequest to the museum.

Stephen Bennett Phillips compiled this chronology from information in Marjorie Leslie Harth, "Robert Hudson Tannahill (1893–1969): Patron and Collector," diss., University of Michigan, 1985.

Duncan Clinch Phillips

A Chronology

Duncan and Marjorie Phillips in the North Library
(now the Music Room of The Phillips Collection) c. 1922.
The paintings are El Greco's *Repentant St. Peter* and Albert
Pinkham Ryder's *Homeward Bound.*

1886
Duncan Clinch Phillips, the second son of Major Duncan Clinch Phillips and Eliza Irwin Laughlin, is born on 26 June in Pittsburgh, Pennsylvania.

1895
Major and Mrs. Phillips spend the winter of 1895–96 in Washington, D.C., and decide they prefer the climate to Pittsburgh's.

1897
Major Phillips buys property at 21st and Q Streets in northwest Washington, D.C., and builds a house designed by Hornblower and Marshall.

1904
Phillips and his older brother, James, enroll at Yale University.

1905
Phillips publishes his first article, "At the Opposite Ends of Art," *Yale Literary Magazine*, 70, June 1905.

1907
Phillips is elected editor of the *Yale Literary Magazine*, serving from 1907 to 1908. He publishes "The Need of Art at Yale" in the June issue.

1908
Phillips and his brother graduate from Yale University.

1911
Phillips takes a trip to Europe during the summer; in Paris he visits the Louvre, the great art dealer Paul Durand-Ruel, and the Musée du Luxembourg.

1913
In December Phillips publishes a stinging review of the Armory Show, "Revolution and Reactions in Painting" (*International Studio*, 51, December 1913), calling it "stupefying in its vulgarity."

1914
While he and his brother are living in New York, Duncan publishes his first book, *The Enchantment of Art*, which includes his *International Studio* review of the Armory Show.

1916
James Phillips writes to his father about his own and Duncan's enthusiasm for paintings and collecting; he requests a yearly stipend for art purchases. A fund is duly established, and many of the early acquisitions are made by James as well as Duncan.

1917
Major Phillips dies suddenly.

1918
James Phillips dies of Spanish influenza thirteen months after his father's death.

Phillips and his mother decide to found the Phillips Memorial Art Gallery, and Phillips begins to build a

collection with this goal. He makes numerous purchases so that, by June 1921, he publishes a checklist of the collection comprising some 230 titles.

1920
McKim, Mead, & White design a skylighted second story over the north wing of the family's residence. This addition becomes the Main Gallery once the museum opens.

1921
Phillips marries Marjorie Acker, a young artist and the niece of the painters Gifford and Reynolds Beal.

In the fall the gallery is quietly opened to the public as the first museum of modern art in America. It is named the Phillips Memorial Art Gallery for only about one year before being renamed the Phillips Memorial Gallery. In 1948 it becomes formally known as The Phillips Gallery, changed to The Phillips Collection in 1961.

1923
Phillips plans an exhibition that includes work by Pierre-Auguste Renoir, Honoré Daumier, Edgar Degas, and Claude Monet.

1925
Phillips inaugurates a series of small one-artist exhibitions in the newly opened Little Gallery, which is used to focus on the work of American artists.

Phillips hangs a group exhibition featuring works by Arthur B. Davies, Kenneth Hayes Miller, and Charles Demuth.

1926

Phillips mounts an exhibition of paintings by nine American artists, including work by Demuth and Charles Sheeler.

Phillips presents an exhibition of paintings by eleven American artists. It includes recent acquisitions of work by Georgia O'Keeffe, Arthur Dove, and Marsden Hartley.

1927

Phillips puts together the exhibition *American Themes by American Painters*, including work by Charles Burchfield and Edward Hopper.

Phillips presents the exhibition *Sensibility and Simplification in Ancient Sculpture and Contemporary Painting*, which includes work by Pierre Bonnard, Paul Cézanne, Georges Seurat, Henri Matisse, and John Marin.

Phillips puts together the exhibition *Intimate Decorations: Chiefly Paintings of Still Life in New Manners by Matisse, Braque, Hartley, Man Ray, Kuhn, O'Keeffe, Knaths and Others.*

Phillips mounts *Leaders of French Art To-Day: Exhibition of Characteristic Works by Matisse, Bonnard, Picasso, Vuillard, Braque, Derain, Segonzac, André, Maillol.*

1928

Phillips presents *A Survey of French Paintings from Chardin to Derain*, which includes work by Daumier, Degas, Vincent van Gogh, and Paul Gauguin.

1929

Phillips is elected to the board of trustees of the Museum of Modern Art, New York.

1930

Phillips puts together the exhibition *Sources of Modernism*, which includes work by El Greco, Bonnard, Daumier, Renoir, Cézanne, Jean-Baptiste-Siméon Chardin, John Constable, Jean-Baptiste-Camille Corot, Pierre Puvis de Chavannes, Edouard Manet, André Derain, and Max Weber.

The Phillips family moves to a new house, and Phillips works on the conversion of the former residence into galleries, offices, and storage space.

1933

Studio House, a combination sales gallery and art school, opens its doors near the gallery.

1938

Phillips puts together *An Exhibition of Watercolors and Oils by Paul Klee*, which includes works from the permanent collection supplemented by loans.

Phillips organizes *Picasso and Marin*, a loan exhibition with forty-six works of art.

1939

Phillips organizes *Toulouse-Lautrec: Exhibition of Drawings, Lithographs, and Posters.*

The museum is a venue for *Georges Braque: Retrospective Exhibition*, organized by the Arts Club of Chicago.

1940

Phillips becomes a trustee and member of the acquisition committee of the National Gallery of Art, Washington, D.C.

The Phillips Memorial Gallery is a venue for *Georges Rouault: Retrospective Loan Exhibition*, organized by the Institute of Modern Art in Boston.

1941

Phillips gives *Willow* (1940) by Dove to MoMA and buys *Advice to a Young Artist* (after 1860) by Daumier as a gift for the National Gallery of Art.

1942

Phillips organizes *Charles Demuth: Exhibition of Watercolors and Oil Paintings*, which includes loans.

Phillips organizes *Paul Klee: A Memorial Exhibition*, which includes loans.

1943

Phillips assembles a loan exhibition of work by Chaim Soutine.

Phillips organizes *John Marin: A Retrospective Loan Exhibition of Paintings.*

Phillips puts together a loan exhibition of paintings by Hartley, which the director of The Detroit Institute of Arts, Dr. William Valentiner, visits.

Phillips presents *Recent Paintings in Gouache by Morris Graves.*

1950

The gallery features *Paintings, Drawings, and Prints by Paul Klee from the Klee Foundation, Berne, Switzerland, with Additions from American Collections*, which comprises 202 works, including 5 paintings from The Phillips Gallery. One of the venues for the exhibition is The Detroit Institute of Arts.

1952

The first comprehensive catalogue of the collection, *The Phillips Collection: A Museum of Modern Art and Its Sources*, is published.

Phillips gives Degas's painting *Ballet Rehearsal* (c. 1885) to the Yale University Art Gallery on the occasion of the laying of the cornerstone for the new gallery.

1960

The new wing of the museum opens to the public.

1961

Phillips continues to introduce the work of contemporary artists in small one-person exhibitions.

1966

Phillips dies on 9 May at his home in Washington, D.C.

Stephen Bennett Phillips excepted this information from Erika Passantino and Sarah Martin, "Chronology," in *Duncan Phillips: Centennial Exhibition* (exhib. cat.,Washington, D.C., The Phillips Collection, 1986), most recently republished in *Master Paintings: The Phillips Collection* (Washington, D.C., The Phillips Collection, 1998).

List of Illustrations

Hilaire-Germain-Edgar Degas

(1834–1917)

Dancers at the Bar, c. 1900

oil on canvas

130.1 × 97.7 cm

(51¼ × 38½ in.)

WASHINGTON, D.C.

THE PHILLIPS COLLECTION

PAGE 83

Hilaire-Germain-Edgar Degas

(1834–1917)

Melancholy, late 1860s

oil on canvas

19 × 24.7 cm

(7½ × 9¾ in.)

WASHINGTON, D.C.

THE PHILLIPS COLLECTION

PAGE 77

Hilaire-Germain-Edgar Degas

(1834–1917)

Spanish Dancer, 1900

bronze

43.2 × 17.2 × 21.9 cm

(17 × 6¾ × 8⁹⁄₁₆ in.)

THE DETROIT INSTITUTE OF ARTS

GIFT OF ROBERT H. TANNAHILL

HALF TITLE (PAGE 1)

Hilaire-Germain-Edgar Degas

(1834–1917)

Violinist and Young Woman,

c. 1871

oil on canvas

46.4 × 55.9 cm

(18¼ × 22 in.)

THE DETROIT INSTITUTE OF ARTS

BEQUEST OF ROBERT H. TANNAHILL

PAGE 82

Hilaire-Germain-Edgar Degas

(1834–1917)

Women Combing Their Hair,

c. 1875–76

oil on paper mounted on

canvas

32.4 × 46.2 cm

(12¾ × 18⅛ in.)

WASHINGTON, D.C.

THE PHILLIPS COLLECTION

PAGE 80

Hilaire-Germain-Edgar Degas

(1834–1917)

Woman with a Headband,

1870–72

oil on canvas

33 × 24.8 cm

(13 × 9¾ in.)

THE DETROIT INSTITUTE OF ARTS

BEQUEST OF ROBERT H. TANNAHILL

PAGE 78

Charles Demuth

(1883–1935)

Monument, Bermuda, 1917

watercolor on paper

35.5 × 25.4 cm

(14 × 10 in.)

WASHINGTON, D.C.

THE PHILLIPS COLLECTION

PAGE 35

Charles Demuth

(1883–1935)

Red Chimneys, 1918

watercolor and graphite on

off-white wove paper

25.6 × 35.6 cm

(10⅛ × 14 in.)

WASHINGTON, D.C.

THE PHILLIPS COLLECTION

PAGE 34

Charles Demuth

(1883–1935)

Trees and Barn, 1917

watercolor on wove paper

25.4 × 35.6 cm

(10 × 14 in.)

THE DETROIT INSTITUTE OF ARTS

BEQUEST OF ROBERT H. TANNAHILL

PAGE 33

Otto Dix

(1891–1969)

*Portrait of the Artist's Son
Ursus,* 1931

watercolor and graphite

pencil on cream wove paper

56.4 × 39 cm

(22¼ × 15⅜ in.)

THE DETROIT INSTITUTE OF ARTS

BEQUEST OF ROBERT H. TANNAHILL

PAGE 103

Lyonel Feininger

(1871–1956)

Quimper, 1932

watercolor and black ink on

laid paper

29.8 × 46.7 cm

(12½ × 18 in.)

THE DETROIT INSTITUTE OF ARTS

BEQUEST OF ROBERT H. TANNAHILL

PAGE 37

Lyonel Feininger

(1871–1956)

Sailboats, 1929

oil on canvas

43.2 × 72.4 cm

(17 × 28½ in.)

THE DETROIT INSTITUTE OF ARTS

GIFT OF ROBERT H. TANNAHILL

PAGE 36

Lyonel Feininger

(1871–1956)

Village, 1927

oil on canvas

42.8 × 72.4 cm

(16⅞ × 28½ in.)

WASHINGTON, D.C.

THE PHILLIPS COLLECTION

PAGE 36

Lyonel Feininger

(1871–1956)

Waterfront, 1942

watercolor and black ink on

paper

29.2 × 45.7 cm

(11½ × 18 in.)

WASHINGTON, D.C.

THE PHILLIPS COLLECTION

PAGE 37

Paul Gauguin

(1848–1903)

Self-Portrait, c. 1893

oil on canvas

46.2 × 38.1 cm

(18³⁄₁₆ × 15 in.)

THE DETROIT INSTITUTE OF ARTS

GIFT OF ROBERT H. TANNAHILL

PAGE 76

Vincent van Gogh

(1853–1890)

Bank of the Oise at Auvers,

1890

oil on canvas

73.3 × 93.7 cm

(28⅞ × 36⅞ in.)

THE DETROIT INSTITUTE OF ARTS

BEQUEST OF ROBERT H. TANNAHILL

PAGE 88

Vincent van Gogh

(1853–1890)

The Diggers, 1889

oil on canvas

65.1 × 50.2 cm

(25⅝ × 19¾ in.)

THE DETROIT INSTITUTE OF ARTS

BEQUEST OF ROBERT H. TANNAHILL

PAGE 89

Vincent van Gogh

(1853–1890)

*Entrance to the Public
Gardens in Arles,* 1888

oil on canvas

72.3 × 90.8 cm

(28½ × 35¾ in.)

WASHINGTON, D.C.

THE PHILLIPS COLLECTION

PAGE 91

Vincent van Gogh

(1853–1890)

The Road Menders, 1889

oil on canvas

73.7 × 92.8

(29 × 36½ in.)

WASHINGTON, D.C.

THE PHILLIPS COLLECTION

PAGE 90

Morris Graves

(born 1910)

Wounded Gull, 1943

gouache on paper

67.6 × 76.8 cm

(26⅝ × 30¼ in.)

WASHINGTON, D.C.

THE PHILLIPS COLLECTION

PAGE 67

Morris Graves
(born 1910)
Wounded Gull, 20th century
watercolor and gouache on paper
67.3 × 77.2 cm
(26½ × 28⅜ in.)
The Detroit Institute of Arts
Bequest of Robert H. Tannahill
page 66

Morris Graves
(born 1910)
Young Gander Ready for Flight, 1952
oil on canvas
121.9 × 84.4 cm
(48 × 33¼ in.)
Washington, D.C.
The Phillips Collection
page 127

George Grosz
(1893–1959)
New York Harbor, 1934
watercolor on off-white wove paper
66.4 × 48.2 cm
(26⅛ × 19 in.)
The Detroit Institute of Arts
Bequest of Robert H. Tannahill
page 38

George Grosz
(1893–1959)
Street in Harlem, 1916
watercolor on paper
62.2 × 43.1 cm
(24½ × 17 in.)
Washington, D.C.
The Phillips Collection
page 39

Marsden Hartley
(1877–1943)
Log Jam, Penobscot Bay, 1940–41
oil on canvas
76.4 × 104 cm
(30 × 40⅞ in.)
The Detroit Institute of Arts
Gift of Robert H. Tannahill
page 58

Marsden Hartley
(1877–1943)
Wood Lot, Maine Woods, 1939
oil on canvas
71.4 × 55.8 cm
(28½ × 22 in.)
Washington, D.C.
The Phillips Collection
page 59

Jean-Auguste-Dominique Ingres
(1780–1867)
Perseus and Andromeda, c. 1819
oil on canvas
19.7 × 16.2 cm
(7¾ × 6⅜ in.)
The Detroit Institute of Arts
Bequest of Robert H. Tannahill
page 84

Jean-Auguste-Dominique Ingres
(1780–1867)
Portrait of Marie Marcoz (later Vicomtesse de Senonnes), 1813
pencil on wove paper
27 × 20.1 cm
(10⅝ × 7⅞ in.)
The Detroit Institute of Arts
Bequest of Robert H. Tannahill
page 85

Jean-Auguste-Dominique Ingres
(1780–1867)
The Small Bather, 1826
oil on canvas
32.7 × 25 cm
(12⅞ × 9⅞ in.)
Washington, D.C.
The Phillips Collection
page 85

Paul Klee
(1879–1940)
Arrival of the Air Steamer, 1921
oil transfer and watercolor on paper with laid texture, mounted on thin cardboard
32.2 × 46 cm
(12¹¹⁄₁₆ × 18⅛ in.)
The Detroit Institute of Arts
Bequest of Robert H. Tannahill
page 40

Paul Klee
(1879–1940)
Arrival of the Jugglers, 1926
oil on incised putty on cardboard mounted on cardboard
17.4 × 27.3 cm
(6⅞ × 10¾ in.)
Washington, D.C.
The Phillips Collection
page 96

Paul Klee
(1879–1940)
Botanical Laboratory, 1928
gouache, watercolor and ink on paper mounted on cardboard
39.3 × 27 cm
(15½ × 10⅝ in.) mount
31.4 × 23.4 cm
(12⅜ × 9¼ in.) image
Washington, D.C.
The Phillips Collection
page 45

Paul Klee
(1879–1940)
Captive Pierrot, 1923
watercolor on heavy paper mounted on gray cardboard
39.7 × 30.2 cm
(15⅝ × 11⅞ in.)
The Detroit Institute of Arts
Bequest of Robert H. Tannahill
page 97

Paul Klee
(1879–1940)
Cathedral, 1924
watercolor and oil washes on paper mounted on cardboard and wood panel
30.1 × 35.5 cm
(11⅞ × 14 in.)
Washington, D.C.
The Phillips Collection
page 40

Paul Klee
(1879–1940)
Garden, 1915
watercolor on paper mounted on thin cardboard
13 × 24.1 cm
(5⅛ × 9½ in.)
The Detroit Institute of Arts
Bequest of Robert H. Tannahill
page 43

Paul Klee
(1879–1940)
Garden Still Life, 1924
oil on paper mounted on cardboard
33.6 × 22.8 cm
(13¼ × 9 in.) mount
28.5 × 19.6 cm
(11¼ × 7¾ in.) image
Washington, D.C.
The Phillips Collection
page 44

Paul Klee
(1879–1940)
Storm over the City, 1925
oil transfer and watercolor on wove paper mounted on thin cardboard; decorative lines in black ink on support above and below mounted sheet
38.4 × 41.9 cm
(15⅛ × 16½ in.)
The Detroit Institute of Arts
Bequest of Robert H. Tannahill
page 41

Paul Klee
(1879–1940)
Tree Nursery, 1929
oil on canvas with incised gesso ground
43.9 × 52.4 cm
(17¼ × 20⅝ in.)
Washington, D.C.
The Phillips Collection
PAGE 41

Paul Klee
(1879–1940)
The Way to the Citadel, 1937
oil on canvas mounted on cardboard
67 × 56.8 cm
(26⅜ × 22⅜ in.)
Washington, D.C.
The Phillips Collection
PAGE 42

Käthe Kollwitz
(1867–1945)
Burial, c. 1903
charcoal and pastel with touches of white chalk on light-brown cardboard or composition board
54.7 × 47.9 cm
(16 × 14 in.)
The Detroit Institute of Arts
Bequest of Robert H. Tannahill
PAGE 65

Käthe Kollwitz
(1867–1945)
Head of a Woman, n.d.
aquatint and etching, 19/50
52.7 × 39.3 cm
(20¾ × 15½ in.) sheet
34.9 × 31.7 cm
(13¾ × 12½ in.) image
Washington, D.C.
The Phillips Collection
Gift of Dwight Clark, *c.* 1934
PAGE 64

Wilhelm Lehmbruck
(1881–1919)
Seated Girl, 1913–14
bronze
27.9 × 44.8 × 14 cm
(11 × 17⅝ × 5½ in.)
The Detroit Institute of Arts
Bequest of Robert H. Tannahill
PAGE 71

Edouard Manet
(1832–1883)
On the Beach, 1873
oil on canvas
40 × 48.9 cm
(15¾ × 19¼ in.)
The Detroit Institute of Arts
Bequest of Robert H. Tannahill
PAGE 87

Franz Marc
(1880–1916)
Animals in a Landscape, 1914
oil on canvas
110.2 × 99.7 cm
(43⅜ × 39¼ in.)
The Detroit Institute of Arts
Gift of Robert H. Tannahill
PAGE 124

Franz Marc
(1880–1916)
Deer in the Forest I, 1913
oil on canvas
100.9 × 104.7 cm
(39¾ × 41¼ in.)
Washington, D.C.
The Phillips Collection
PAGE 125

John Marin
(1870–1953)
Mt. Chocorua – White Mountains, 1926
watercolor and graphite on paper
42.5 × 54.6 cm
(16¾ × 21½ in.)
Washington, D.C.
The Phillips Collection
PAGE 16

John Marin
(1870–1953)
Near Great Barrington, 1925
watercolor and graphite on paper
38.4 × 47.9 cm
(15⅛ × 18⅞ in.)
Washington, D.C.
The Phillips Collection
PAGE 17

John Marin
(1870–1953)
New Mexican Landscape, near Taos, 1930
watercolor on paper
35.2 × 47.6 cm
(13⅞ × 18¾ in.)
The Detroit Institute of Arts
Bequest of Robert H. Tannahill
PAGE 15

Henri Matisse
(1869–1954)
Coffee, 1916
oil on canvas
100.7 × 65.4 cm
(39⅝ × 25¾ in.)
The Detroit Institute of Arts
Bequest of Robert H. Tannahill
PAGE 99

Henri Matisse
(1869–1954)
Interior with Egyptian Curtain, 1948
oil on canvas
116.3 × 89.2 cm
(45¾ × 35⅛ in.)
Washington, D.C.
The Phillips Collection
PAGE 130

Henri Matisse
(1869–1954)
Poppies, c. 1919
oil on canvas
100.7 × 81.3 cm
(39⅝ × 32 in.)
The Detroit Institute of Arts
Bequest of Robert H. Tannahill
PAGE 131

Henri Matisse
(1869–1954)
Seated Female Nude, n.d.
black crayon on paper
62.9 × 47.6 cm
(24 13/16 × 18¾ in.)
The Detroit Institute of Arts
Bequest of Robert H. Tannahill
PAGE 98

Henri Matisse
(1869–1954)
Seated Nude, 1909
bronze
29.2 × 15.6 × 21.6 cm
(11½ × 6⅛ × 8½ in.)
The Detroit Institute of Arts
Bequest of Robert H. Tannahill
PAGE 72

Henri Matisse
(1869–1954)
Studio, Quai St. Michel, 1916
oil on canvas
147.9 × 116.8 cm
(58¼ × 46 in.)
Washington, D.C.
The Phillips Collection
PAGE 133

Henri Matisse
(1869–1954)
Untitled (Seated Nude), 1908
ink on paper
27 × 20.9 cm
(10⅝ × 8¼ in.)
Washington, D.C.
The Phillips Collection
Gift of Marjorie Phillips, 1984
PAGE 98

Paula Modersohn-Becker
(1876–1907)
Old Peasant Woman, c. 1905
oil on canvas
75.6 × 57.8 cm
(29¾ × 22¾ in.)
The Detroit Institute of Arts
Gift of Robert H. Tannahill
PAGE 79

Amedeo Modigliani

(1884–1920)

A Man, 20th century

oil on canvas

46 × 38.1 cm

(18⅛ × 15 in.)

THE DETROIT INSTITUTE OF ARTS

BEQUEST OF ROBERT H. TANNAHILL

PAGE 101

Amedeo Modigliani

(1884–1920)

Elena Povolozky, 1917

oil on canvas

64.6 × 48.5 cm

(25½ × 19⅛ in.)

WASHINGTON, D.C.

THE PHILLIPS COLLECTION

PAGE 102

Amedeo Modigliani

(1884–1920)

Young Man with a Cap,

20th century

oil on canvas

61 × 37.8 cm

(24 × 14⅞ in.)

THE DETROIT INSTITUTE OF ARTS

BEQUEST OF ROBERT H. TANNAHILL

PAGE 100

Piet Mondrian

(1870–1944)

Self-Portrait, c. 1900

oil on canvas, mounted on

hardboard

50.7 × 39.3 cm

(20 × 15½ in.)

WASHINGTON, D.C.

THE PHILLIPS COLLECTION

PAGE 76

Henry Moore

(1898–1986)

Family Group, 1946

bronze

44.3 × 33.2 × 22 cm

(17½ × 13 × 8⅝ in.)

WASHINGTON, D.C.

THE PHILLIPS COLLECTION

PAGE 115

Henry Moore

(1898–1986)

Family Group No. 2, 1944

watercolor over pencil

and ink

46.4 × 36.2 cm

(18¼ × 14⅛ in.)

THE DETROIT INSTITUTE OF ARTS

BEQUEST OF ROBERT H. TANNAHILL

PAGE 115

Henry Moore

(1898–1986)

Figures in a Setting, 1942

wax crayon, watercolor, pen

and ink, white gouache, and

graphite on wove paper

36.5 × 51.6 cm

(14⅜ × 20¼ in.)

WASHINGTON, D.C.

THE PHILLIPS COLLECTION

PAGE 114

Otto Mueller

(1874–1930)

Two Bathers, 1928–30

crayon, pastel, watercolor,

and brush and black ink on

off-white wove paper

52 × 68.5 cm

(20½ × 27 in.)

THE DETROIT INSTITUTE OF ARTS

BEQUEST OF ROBERT H. TANNAHILL

PAGE 103

Emil Nolde

(1867–1956)

Tulips and Bird, c. 1920

watercolor on Japanese paper

34.9 × 48.6 cm

(13¾ × 19⅛ in.)

THE DETROIT INSTITUTE OF ARTS

BEQUEST OF ROBERT H. TANNAHILL

PAGE 126

Pablo Picasso

(1881–1973)

Abstraction, Biarritz, 1918

oil on canvas

35.5 × 27.3 cm

(14¼ × 10¾ in.)

WASHINGTON, D.C.

THE PHILLIPS COLLECTION

PAGE 129

Pablo Picasso

(1881–1973)

The Blue Room, 1901

oil on canvas

50.4 × 61.5 cm

(19⅞ × 24¼ in.)

WASHINGTON, D.C.

THE PHILLIPS COLLECTION

PAGE 108

Pablo Picasso

(1881–1973)

Bottle of Anis del Mono, 1915

oil on canvas

46 × 54.6 cm

(18⅛ × 21½ in.)

THE DETROIT INSTITUTE OF ARTS

BEQUEST OF ROBERT H. TANNAHILL

PAGE 128

Pablo Picasso

(1881–1973)

Head of a Harlequin, 1905

oil on canvas

40.6 × 33 cm

(16 × 13 in.)

THE DETROIT INSTITUTE OF ARTS

BEQUEST OF ROBERT H. TANNAHILL

PAGE 109

Pablo Picasso

(1881–1973)

Woman's Head, 1945

lithograph, 50/50

30.8 × 23.4 cm

(12⅛ × 9¼ in.)

WASHINGTON, D.C.

THE PHILLIPS COLLECTION

PAGE 104

Pablo Picasso

(1881–1973)

Melancholy Woman, 1902

oil on canvas

100 × 69.2 cm

(39⅜ × 27¼ in.)

THE DETROIT INSTITUTE OF ARTS

BEQUEST OF ROBERT H. TANNAHILL

PAGE 107

Pablo Picasso

(1881–1973)

Seated Woman, 1924

lithograph, 11/50

38.1 × 27.9 cm

(15 × 11 in.) sheet

29.8 × 21.5 cm

(11¾ × 8½ in.) image

WASHINGTON, D.C.

THE PHILLIPS COLLECTION

GIFT OF MARJORIE PHILLIPS, 1984

PAGE 104

Pablo Picasso

(1881–1973)

Three Bathers, Juan-les-Pins,

1920

graphite pencil on wove paper

27.3 × 42.1 cm

(10⅝ × 13¾ in.)

THE DETROIT INSTITUTE OF ARTS

BEQUEST OF ROBERT H. TANNAHILL

PAGE 105

Pablo Picasso

(1881–1973)

*Woman Seated in an

Armchair*, 1923

oil on canvas

130.2 × 97.2 cm

(51¼ × 38¼ in.)

THE DETROIT INSTITUTE OF ARTS

BEQUEST OF ROBERT H. TANNAHILL

PAGE 106

Pierre-Auguste Renoir

(1841–1919)

*The Luncheon of the Boating

Party*, 1880–81

oil on canvas

130 × 201 cm

(51¼ × 69⅛ in.)

WASHINGTON, D.C.

THE PHILLIPS COLLECTION

PAGE 21

Pierre-Auguste Renoir

(1841–1919)

The Palm Tree, 1902

oil on canvas

46.4 × 55.6 cm

(18¼ × 21⅞ in.)

THE DETROIT INSTITUTE OF ARTS

BEQUEST OF ROBERT H. TANNAHILL

PAGE 22

Pierre-Auguste Renoir

(1841–1919)

Seated Bather, 1903–06

oil on canvas

116.2 × 88.9 cm

(45¾ × 35 in.)

THE DETROIT INSTITUTE OF ARTS

BEQUEST OF ROBERT H. TANNAHILL

PAGE 81

Diego Rivera

(1886–1957)

Portrait of Robert H. Tannahill, 1932

oil on canvas

88.3 × 69.9 cm

(34¾ × 27½ in.)

THE DETROIT INSTITUTE OF ARTS

BEQUEST OF ROBERT H. TANNAHILL

PAGE 123

Diego Rivera

(1886–1957)

Still Life with Carafe, Knife, and Chestnuts, 1918

pencil on paper

31.4 × 23.3 cm

(12⅜ × 9³⁄₁₆ in.)

THE DETROIT INSTITUTE OF ARTS

BEQUEST OF ROBERT H. TANNAHILL

PAGE 132

Auguste Rodin

(1840–1917)

Baudelaire, 1898

bronze

22.5 × 20 × 22.9 cm

(8⅞ × 7⅞ × 9 in.)

THE DETROIT INSTITUTE OF ARTS

BEQUEST OF ROBERT H. TANNAHILL

PAGE 73

Auguste Rodin

(1840–1917)

Brother and Sister, 1890

bronze

38.1 × 17.7 × 15.8 cm

(15 × 7 × 6¼ in.)

WASHINGTON, D.C.

THE PHILLIPS COLLECTION

GIFT FROM THE ESTATE OF

KATHERINE S. DREIER, 1953

PAGE 73

Georges Rouault

(1871–1958)

The Clown, c. 1907

gouache and oil on board

57.2 × 50.8 cm

(22½ × 20 in.)

THE DETROIT INSTITUTE OF ARTS

BEQUEST OF ROBERT H. TANNAHILL

PAGE 110

Georges Rouault

(1871–1958)

Standing Nude, 1909

watercolor and oil on cardboard

99.1 × 63.2 cm

(35⅞ × 24⅞ in.)

THE DETROIT INSTITUTE OF ARTS

BEQUEST OF ROBERT H. TANNAHILL

PAGE 111

Georges Rouault

(1871–1958)

Tragic Landscape, 1930

ink and gouache on paper

47.6 × 59.6 cm

(18¾ × 23½ in.)

WASHINGTON, D.C.

THE PHILLIPS COLLECTION

PAGE 49

Henri Rousseau

(1844–1910)

Notre Dame, 1909

oil on canvas

32.7 × 40.9 cm

(12⅞ × 16⅛ in.)

WASHINGTON, D.C.

THE PHILLIPS COLLECTION

PAGE 46

Henri Rousseau

(1844–1910)

The Environs of Paris, 1909

oil on canvas

46.4 × 55.6 cm

(18¼ × 21⅞ in.)

THE DETROIT INSTITUTE OF ARTS

BEQUEST OF ROBERT H. TANNAHILL

PAGE 47

Henri Rousseau

(1844–1910)

Vase of Flowers, 19ᵗʰ–20ᵗʰ century

oil on canvas

33.3 × 24.1 cm

(13⅛ × 9½ in.)

THE DETROIT INSTITUTE OF ARTS

BEQUEST OF ROBERT H. TANNAHILL

PAGE 61

Karl Schmidt-Rottluff

(1884–1976)

Blossoming Trees, 1930–33

watercolor and brush and black ink over black crayon on white wove paper

50 × 70 cm

(20 × 27½ in.)

THE DETROIT INSTITUTE OF ARTS

BEQUEST OF ROBERT H. TANNAHILL

PAGE 48

Georges Seurat

(1859–1891)

View of Le Crotoy from Upstream, 1889

oil on canvas

70.5 × 86.7 cm

(27¾ × 34⅛ in.)

THE DETROIT INSTITUTE OF ARTS

BEQUEST OF ROBERT H. TANNAHILL

PAGE 27

Chaim Soutine

(1893–1943)

Little Girl, 20ᵗʰ century

oil on canvas

54.9 × 43.2 cm

(21⅝ × 17 in.)

THE DETROIT INSTITUTE OF ARTS

BEQUEST OF ROBERT H. TANNAHILL

PAGE 112

Chaim Soutine

(1893–1943)

Woman in Profile, 1937

oil on canvas

46.6 × 27.6 cm

(18⅜ × 10⅞ in.)

WASHINGTON, D.C.

THE PHILLIPS COLLECTION

PAGE 113

Henri de Toulouse-Lautrec

(1864–1901)

At the Circus, 1899

black chalk, crayon, and gray wash on wove paper

25.2 × 35.6 cm

(9¹⁵⁄₁₆ × 14 in.)

THE DETROIT INSTITUTE OF ARTS

BEQUEST OF ROBERT H. TANNAHILL

PAGE 95

Henri de Toulouse-Lautrec

(1864–1901)

La Loge: A Performance of "Faust," 1896

lithograph

38.1 × 27.9 cm

(15 × 11 in.)

WASHINGTON, D.C.

THE PHILLIPS COLLECTION

PAGE 95

Henri de Toulouse-Lautrec

(1864–1901)

Miss May Belfort, state 1, 1895

color lithograph

54.6 × 42.2 cm

(21½ × 16⅝ in.) image

WASHINGTON, D.C.

THE PHILLIPS COLLECTION

PAGE 95

Index

Page numbers in *italic* refer to illustrations